The Glass Anvil

POETS ON POETRY

DAVID LEHMAN, GENERAL EDITOR

Allen Grossman *The Long Schoolroom*
Jonathan Holden
   Guns and Boyhood in America
Andrew Hudgins *The Glass Anvil*
Carol Muske *Women and Poetry*

A. R. Ammons *Set in Motion*
Douglas Crase *AMERIFIL.TXT*
Suzanne Gardinier
   A World That Will Hold All the People
Kenneth Koch *The Art of Poetry*

DONALD HALL, FOUNDING EDITOR

Martin Lammon, Editor
   Written in Water, Written in Stone
Philip Booth *Trying to Say It*
Joy Harjo *The Spiral of Memory*
Richard Tillinghast
   Robert Lowell's Life and Work
Marianne Boruch *Poetry's Old Air*
Alan Williamson *Eloquence and Mere Life*
Mary Kinzie *The Judge Is Fury*
Thom Gunn *Shelf Life*
Robert Creeley *Tales Out of School*
Fred Chappell *Plow Naked*
Gregory Orr *Richer Entanglements*
Daniel Hoffman *Words to Create a World*
David Lehman *The Line Forms Here*
   · *The Big Question*
Jane Miller *Working Time*
Amy Clampitt *Predecessors, Et Cetera*
Peter Davison
   One of the Dangerous Trades
William Meredith
   Poems Are Hard to Read
Tom Clark *The Poetry Beat*
William Matthews *Curiosities*
Charles Wright *Halflife* · *Quarter Notes*
Weldon Kees
   Reviews and Essays, 1936–55
Tess Gallagher *A Concert of Tenses*
Charles Simic *The Uncertain Certainty*
   · *Wonderful Words, Silent Truth*
   · *The Unemployed Fortune-Teller*
Anne Sexton *No Evil Star*
John Frederick Nims *A Local Habitation*

Donald Justice *Platonic Scripts*
Robert Hayden *Collected Prose*
Hayden Carruth *Effluences from the*
   Sacred Caves · *Suicides and Jazzers*
John Logan *A Ballet for the Ear*
Alicia Ostriker
   Writing Like a Woman
Marvin Bell *Old Snow Just Melting*
James Wright *Collected Prose*
Marge Piercy
   Parti-Colored Blocks for a Quilt
John Haines *Living Off the Country*
Philip Levine *Don't Ask*
Louis Simpson *A Company of Poets*
   · *The Character of the Poet*
   · *Ships Going into the Blue*
Richard Kostelanetz
   The Old Poetries and the New
David Ignatow *Open Between Us*
Robert Francis *Pot Shots at Poetry*
Robert Bly *Talking All Morning*
Diane Wakoski *Toward a New Poetry*
Maxine Kumin *To Make a Prairie*
Donald Davie *Trying to Explain*
William Stafford
   Writing the Australian Crawl ·
   You Must Revise Your Life
Galway Kinnell
   Walking Down the Stairs
Donald Hall *Goatfoot Milktongue*
   Twinbird · *The Weather for Poetry* ·
   Poetry and Ambition · *Death to the*
   Death of Poetry

Andrew Hudgins

The Glass Anvil

Ann Arbor

THE UNIVERSITY OF MICHIGAN PRESS

For Randall Curb

Copyright © by the University of Michigan 1997
All rights reserved
Published in the United States of America by
The University of Michigan Press
Manufactured in the United States of America
♾ Printed on acid-free paper

2000   1999   1998   1997   4   3   2   1

A CIP catalog record for this book is available from the British Library.

Library of Congress Cataloging-in-Publication Data

Hudgins, Andrew.
     The glass anvil / Andrew Hudgins.
        p.   cm. — (Poets on poetry)
     ISBN 0-472-09615-X (cloth). — ISBN 0-472-06615-3 (pbk.)
     1. Hudgins, Andrew—Interviews.   2. Hudgins, Andrew—
Authorship.   3. Poetics.   4. Poetry.   I. Title.   II. Series.
PS3558.U288G5   1997
811'.54—dc21
     [B]   96-49139
                                                                    CIP

Contents

All I had was some blue paint; however, I intended to draw the chase. Having soon painted a blue boy astride a blue horse and some blue dogs as well, I did not know for certain whether one might draw a blue hare and ran off to the study to consult Papa. Papa was reading, and in reply to my question: "Are there any blue hares?" replied without raising his eyes: "Yes, my boy, there are." Returning to the round table, I painted a blue hare, then decided to change the blue hare into a bush. I was not pleased by the bush, either; I changed it into a tree, the tree into a haystack, the haystack into a cloud and, in the end, made such a blue mess on the sheet of paper that I tore it up in a pique and went off to nap in the wing chair.

—Leo Tolstoy

I

Reader to Writer

Reader to Writer

At a party at Stanford University, where I was a Stegner fellow in poetry, a friend suddenly asked with abrupt and aggressive intensity, "When you were growing up were there books in the house?"

"No," I said, "not really."

That was true for him too, he said, when he was growing up in an Italian neighborhood in Providence, Rhode Island. Like me and many of the writers I knew there, most of them from poor or middle-class families, he was, I suppose, amazed and gratified to find himself at Stanford, and a little touchy about it.

"Not really" was the most accurate answer I could come up with under the pressure of the moment, the unexpected question in front of friends, and though my answer was more true than not, there were in fact some books that moved with us from house to house as my father was transferred by the Air Force. It's not that my parents were against books or afraid of them; they weren't. They simply saw no need to pay money for something that would only be used once and that could be checked out of the library for free. If anything, they believed that reading was an unalloyed good, and Mom started teaching me early. The year before I began first grade, she called the school board in Goldsboro, North Carolina—my father was stationed at nearby Seymour Johnson Air Force Base—and bullied them into letting her buy copies of all the first-grade readers. Sitting on her lap, following her index finger as it moved from word to word, I stumbled through the listless adventures of Dick, Jane, Spot, and

From *Contemporary Authors: Autobiography Series,* ed. Joyce Nakamura, vol. 21 (Detroit: Gale Research, 1995), 101–18.

Puff, who spent their lives looking and seeing. Occasionally they ran, but mostly they looked and they saw. By the time I began first grade, I knew the books backward and forward. I'm not sure I could read them so much as I had simply memorized them from countless hours of repeating each word as my mother's red fingernail pressed a faint crescent into the white space under it. When students in other reading groups got stuck on a word, I'd lift my head from whatever work I was doing at my desk and shout the answer, out of the sheer pleasure of knowing it and out of impatience too, that the story had stalled. For some reason, the teacher tolerated my disruptions, perhaps not wanting to blunt my enthusiasm.

When we moved into on-base housing the next year, I could ride my bike to the base library. Base libraries are usually spartan places—cramped, dark, and staffed by volunteers who loan well-worn, donated books with floppy spines. The library at Seymour Johnson was one of the spartan ones, but I know that only in retrospect. It was the first library I'd ever seen and for me it held treasures. It contained about one-third of the books in the Hardy Boys series. Like ancient documents, the books were torn, creased, stained, annotated, mildewy, and occasionally missing pages entirely, but the library would let me take them home for two weeks at a time! And then, if necessary, I could check them out for two more weeks! I even enjoyed the dignified transactions that transpired if I kept the books past the due date and had to count out a dime or two to the librarian, who would expiate my shame by counting back unsmilingly the pennies I was due as change.

At home, though, the books were mine, not the library's. I could pile them up, hoard them, save them for later, or pitch myself into the heroics of F. W. Dixon's Hardy Boys—and I noticed for the first time how, as I neared the conclusion of each book, I'd read more and more slowly, drawing out the pleasure, lingering as long as I could in the world I did not want to leave. Lying belly-down on my bed with my head hanging over the side and the book cracked open on the floor, I was so deeply engaged in the world created by F. W. Dixon that I wouldn't hear my mother calling me to supper and she'd come back and say, good-naturedly, "Hey, Mister Anti-social! Come join the rest of the family." I can still summon, though weakly through the decades, the dismay I felt when I discovered that F. W. Dixon was not really the author of the Hardy Boys books but a pseudonym for many different writers working to a formula. I felt that some tacit agreement had been violated, some faith betrayed. I'd trusted F. W. Dixon, merged my nervous system with his sentences and stories until I was oblivious to the world outside them, and then I found out he didn't exist. O cruel and faithless F. W. Dixon! You should have made me more suspicious of reading than you did. But since I had no doubts about my love for Frank and Joe Hardy, whose lives were so much more interesting and so much more understandable than my own, I yielded quickly to pragmatism: "Oh, so that's how it's done. Well, who cares as long as I get to read the books."

I learned early that reading, which I saw as a pure pleasure, was seen by my parents as work, a virtue in and of itself, something to be encouraged, a form of self-improvement, and I shamelessly exploited that chasm between our perceptions. If Mom shouted back down the hall "Andrew, what are you doing?" and I answered "nothing," I'd end up scrubbing the baseboards, mowing the lawn, or peeling carrots. But if I shouted back "reading," the odds were better than fifty-fifty that I'd get out of work. Reading was more important than baseboards, the lawn, or carrots, even though I knew—and kept the guilty knowledge to myself—that I was only reading the Hardy Boys, sports biographies, books about noble and preternaturally intelligent collies—books that had no merit other than unadulterated escapism except that they could reveal the pleasures of reading itself.

I read purely to escape, not for knowledge or wisdom, not to strengthen my reading skills or deepen my psychological acuity. A shy child, miserable and self-conscious, I plunged myself into imagined worlds where I could be a Hardy Boy or young King Arthur. Though I couldn't know it then, I was assuming, as readers do, the hero's understanding and mastery of his simplified world. In my own life, though constantly aware of how little I grasped my parents' expectations of me, I was painfully aware too of how short I fell of those expectations. My parents were natural athletes. Their golf and bowling trophies were jumbled on the shelves. Before going in the navy, Dad had begun college at Georgia Southern University on a football scholarship, and he went from the navy to West Point, where he played football on the same team as Doc Blanchard and Glenn Davis. I believe he was a drop-kicker, but I'm not sure. He never talked about it. My mother was, if anything, a better athlete than he. They understood sports, enjoyed them, excelled at them, and assumed without question that I would too. Every year I played baseball, football, basketball. I bowled. One of the more courageous acts I performed as a boy was when at twelve or thirteen, after weeks of agonized planning, I told my parents I didn't want to play Little League anymore because I was tired of standing out in right field praying that no fly balls would be hit in my direction. "Okay, if that's what you want," they said. And life, to my surprise, went on. The only sport I stuck with was judo because my father knew nothing about it and therefore couldn't stand on the sidelines yelling instructions that were soon followed by frustrated recriminations about my failure to follow the instructions. But unlike sports, which belonged to them, reading was mine. They didn't understand it and, therefore, in their sentimental view of it as almost always good, they didn't try to direct it. With only a few exceptions, books were mine and I, no matter how unformed by taste, could read what I wanted to read. I was free to pursue my pleasures.

Only a couple of times did my parents institute prohibitions about what I could read. When I was eleven or twelve, superhero comics, my favorites, were banned. I think it was because superheroes are more powerful than Christ and are therefore anti-Christian, my father being from time to time overinfluenced briefly by sermons he'd heard. All my *Batman, Superman, Green Lantern, Wonder Woman* comics, even my treasured copies of *Spiderman,* were pitched, and for awhile my brothers and I were permitted only insipid "baby" comics like *Richie Rich, Mighty Mouse, Baby Huey,* and *Archie.* And we were encouraged to read a two-volume, comic book version of the Bible that my parents bought. In comic book form I enjoyed the Old Testament more than the New. Floods, pillars of salt, Eve and the serpent make, for a twelve year old, a more intriguing story than pictures of a leper clutching at the hem of Jesus' robe, especially if the twelve year old isn't sure what a leper is. I was fascinated by the picture of Absalom hanging by his hair from a tree limb while his murderers taunted him, though I believe the book, to spare the sensibilities of us young readers, obscured the fact that he was killed. Soon, with nothing being said, the ban on comics was abandoned and, instead of going to our friends' houses and reading their tainted comics, we could stand in the PX and honestly wheedle Mom into "wasting good money," as she put it, on *Spiderman* or *The Fantastic Four*.

A year or two later I was forbidden to read any James Bond books because the movie version of *Goldfinger* came out in 1964 and received a tremendous amount of lubricious publicity for its sex scenes and its "Bond girls" with names like Pussy Galore. I knew it would be pointless even to ask permission to see the movie but I resented being told what I couldn't read. I went to the base library, sat in a corner out of sight, and over a few months systematically worked my way through the Ian Fleming oeuvre. Even after I'd become thoroughly bored with the Bond books, I kept on reading till I'd read them all. These were the only times my father ever restricted my reading though he certainly would have done it again if he'd discovered the copy of *My Secret Life* that, in high school, I smuggled into the house and kept hidden behind the neatly fronted-up books on my bookshelf. My parents rarely asked what I was reading and I didn't tell them. If they did ask, I'd tell them the title and nothing else.

This strategy generally worked pretty well. But when I was fourteen, *The Green Berets,* a huge best-seller, came out in paperback and I was able to talk my parents into buying it for me because my father assumed it would glorify the Green Berets. I read the book and then passed it on to my father, who wanted to see what it said about Vietnam, where within eighteen months he'd be sent, something that he must have suspected would happen.

A week or so later, he came into my room, shut the door, sat on the side of the bed, and said softly, "I want to talk to you." He was clearly upset, struggling for words, and I was frightened, wondering what I'd done wrong. A gentle approach like that usually meant a long and wrenching heart-to-heart about why I wasn't "working up to my potential" at school or how I would have to step up and be more of a man around the house and more helpful to my mother while he was on TDY (temporary duty out of town). He told me he'd read the book and he was sorry he'd let me read such filth. "Listen," he said, "I just want you to know that people don't really live like that. These writers just make a lot of wild stuff up to sell books." He insisted on the point and insisted that I agree with him that "people don't really live like that." I had no idea what he was talking about. Was he talking about the war? About killing? But of course people killed each other in war. He was there, he said, anytime I needed to talk about these things, okay? I said okay, and he slapped me affectionately on the thigh and stood up. After I'd agreed again that people don't really live like that and after he'd left, I realized he meant sex. That people don't really have sex outside marriage. I didn't know who was right, Dad or the book; to me, they both offered views of the world I had no way of judging. But the book, though I suspected it of embellishment and sensationalism, held out a richer, more complex, more frightening and therefore more compelling world than my father did.

Educational reading, on the other hand, was encouraged even though Mom and Dad resisted the blandishments of door-to-door encyclopedia salesmen after twice sitting through the entire *Encyclopedia Britannica* spiel. And I, the object of the skirmish, hunched in a corner of the couch and listened as the earnest middle-aged man and later the even more earnest young one presented themselves as vitally interested in my education while respectfully insinuating that my parents, though they of course thought they too were concerned about my welfare, were perhaps not as totally committed to it as one might hope if they denied me my own personal set of the *Encyclopedia Britannica.* Immense and frightening, the *Britannica* looked to me like something I'd never comprehend, and I understood immediately that it would be an expenditure I'd hear about every time I brought home a C on my report card, and since my report card consisted mostly of C's I knew I'd become uncomfortably knowledgeable about the pricing structures and financing procedures of the Britannica corporation. The huge set of books would squat on its own bookcase in the living room like a dark unsatisfiable troll called Obligation. So before my parents turned to me and asked if I really needed such an expensive thing at home when they'd be happy to take me to the base library anytime I needed to go and anyway there was a set of Brittanica in the school library, wasn't there, I was already praying for this cup to pass.

But the sales pitch about how they'd be cheating their kids if we didn't have free and easy access to an encyclopedia must have hit home with Mom. For the only time I remember, she didn't do the weekly shopping at the commissary on base; instead she went to a local grocery store that each week sold a different child's encyclopedia volume for ninety-nine cents with a minimum purchase of twenty-five dollars. We ended up with, I think, nine of the ten volumes. Though I no longer remember the name of that encyclopedia, I loved those cheap books. Skipping from subject to subject, I read randomly: Tea, Texas, Wisconsin, Coal. I'd take a volume into the bathroom, lock the door, sit on the commode, and read for hours. I tried to keep one volume open on the toilet tank so I could read it while I stood peeing. With two brothers then and later three, I relished privacy because it was hard to come by. Sometimes I'd lock myself in the bathroom, lie on the cold floor and read. After awhile, Mom would pound on the door and say, "Boy, did you fall in?" For some reason, I was fascinated with the maps of states and foreign countries, which were marked with little symbols showing what parts of Texas grew cotton and what parts of Germany and France were rich producers of bauxite. And because we owned Volume 1, *A–Ch*, I knew bauxite was the principal ore of aluminum and that it was named after Les Baux, the place in southern France where it was first discovered. A year ago I found a complete set of those encyclopedias in an antique store in Sunbury, Ohio, and it took a great deal of self-control not to spend thirty dollars and, by that act of sentimental ransom, assure myself of disappointment. I loved them truly when I was a boy, but then is then and now is for books, mature loves. To buy those encyclopedias and read them now would be like trying to fall in love with a twelve-year-old girl—acceptable when you're ten or twelve yourself, or even thirteen, but morally repugnant when you're forty-three.

I dashed from book to book without plan or method. In the twelve-foot-by-twelve-foot library at Del Rosa Elementary School in San Bernardino, California, where we lived for the three years my father was stationed at Norton AFB, a boy standing next to me as I tried to choose a book revealed his method: "I go to the last page and if the last word is a good word I'll read the book."

He tipped a book off the shelf and flipped to the end. "See, this book ends with 'eagle.' That's a really good word. I'll read this one."

It sounded like a good plan, but though I tried, I couldn't make it work. To me, *all* the words looked like good ones. "Faith," "Red," "die," "should"—I couldn't judge which word possessed the greatest inherent virtue. I simply lugged home piles of books, and if I got past page two, I finished the book. But I did get on riffs. Paul Bunyon led to Pecos Bill, who led to Barnacle Bill, who begat Railroad Bill, who begat John Henry and other tall-tale heroes I've forgotten.

At Del Vallejo Junior High the next year I signed up for a class in library work, and I got to do such temporarily interesting chores as putting book covers on the books, burning call numbers on spines, and gluing card pockets on the inside back covers. But after I'd performed these crafts twenty or thirty times, I volunteered to do the shelving because I would toss the books back in place quickly and have plenty of time left to find a chair outside the librarian's line of sight and read about Kit Carson and Jim Bridger. Then, because they had a lot of grotesque details about massacres and cannibalism, I began to tear through colonial captivity narratives and books about the frontier Indian wars. At Del Vallejo I also read my first best-seller, and it would be hard for me to exaggerate how proud I was to be reading an adult book that seriously engaged adult subjects: *Seven Days in May,* an edgy and, to my mind, sophisticated story of nuclear tit-for-tat with Moscow and New York being wiped out.

The books we owned and that traveled with us from house to rented house included the Bible, which I didn't really consider a book because it was holy, the Bible comics, the children's encyclopedia, and about twenty books that appeared in a magical thud followed by several magical dribbles as a result of a short-lived membership my parents took in the Book-of-the-Month Club. They'd signed up for one of those twelve-books-for-a-dollar deals and then bought the minimum number of books required to discharge their obligation, something I did myself a couple of years ago with the Record-of-the-Month Club—just so you'll know I'm not sneering at them. And why would I sneer at a legal and ethical transaction that brought under our roof a couple of Frank Yerby novels that I always meant to read but never did, a superb book of hillbilly stories called *Tall Tales from the High Hills,* and perhaps the greatest book ever written, a book even more sophisticated than *Seven Days in May* because it included literary and historical information: Bennett Cerf's *Laugh Treasury,* which collected four of Cerf's earlier books into a Bennett Cerf magnum opus.

I was enthralled. For hours at a time I flipped through the thick books and read the short sketches, nothing longer than a couple of pages and most of them only a few sentences—cultural and historical anecdotes, ghost stories, jokes, odds and ends of wit. The anecdotes were heavy on stories about twentieth-century American writers—Hemingway, Fitzgerald, Faulkner, and the Algonquin wits, not a one of whom I'd heard, but Cerf's blithe certainty that these writers required no introduction made me feel included, welcome, special, even as he bewildered me. Cerf's unpatronizing assumption of shared knowledge gave his literary snippets weight and significance, and made me feel as if I were not just glimpsing, but participating in an alien and superior world. To me, a sheltered boy, poor student, and worse athlete, it was an insider's view of a sophisticated and clever life that I, as a reader, would join on privileged terms by assuming Cerf's insider status.

Long before I'd ever read a word written by Ernest Hemingway, I knew that his contract with Scribner's stipulated that no word in his manuscripts would be altered without his consent. I know because Bennett Cerf told me that Maxwell Perkins, when reading the manuscript of *Death in the Afternoon,* came across the word "fuck" and, knowing he couldn't print it, jotted the word down on his list of "What to Do Today," so he would remember to discuss alternatives with Hemingway. When Perkins's secretary saw the note, she exclaimed, "Does a secretary have to remind her boss to do *everything*?" Pretty racy stuff. But I must have read the anecdote ten times over three years before I finally understood it because Cerf was of course working under nearly the same publishing constraints as Perkins. He identifies the troublesome word only as "a four-letter Anglo-Saxon word beginning with 'f' "—a description that completely foxed me, though at first I would have been just as much in the dark if he'd used the word outright. And if I couldn't grasp "fuck," I couldn't hope to grasp the distinction between "like" and "love" that Cerf credits to William Faulkner, who quotes a young lady from Mississippi as explaining, "If I like 'em, I lets 'em. If I loves 'em, I helps." But sex was not the only thing I was blind to. Though I've read that anecdote many times, not until today, rereading it to refresh my memory, did I register the casual and unexamined racism of the time that's implicit in the dialect.

Ignorance did not detract from my fascination with these stories. Far from it. If anything, the fact that I did not wholly understand them was intrinsic to my fascination; it's what drew me back to them as I struggled to justify Cerf's faith in our shared knowingness. And what, in Cerf's stories, I understood only in part, and that part only vaguely, outweighed the little I did understand fully in my own life, which was by its nature mundane. Cerf made me feel like I could understand the clash of the titans. From Cerf, I knew that Hemingway had confronted Max Eastman for referring to him in print as the leader of the "false-hair-on-the chest" school of writing. Cerf is vague on what happened next but gives the impression that violence ensued. The anecdote is illustrated by a caricature of belligerent Hemingway, his massive chest and simian arms covered with a thick pelt of curly black hair, while a caricature of scrawny, cowed Max Eastman pulls one curly hair straight out from Hemingway's sternum and stares at it, bemused. Seeing these complex people reduced to this silly story and sillier drawing, I felt superior to both the macho strutting novelist and the weasely critic who had chosen the wrong person to abuse from what he took to be the safe distance of print.

I didn't know who Ernest Hemingway was, I still don't really know who Max Eastman was, and I had only a rough idea what hair-on-the-chest implied, but I loved Bennett Cerf for assuming

I knew as much as he did, or that I would if I just kept reading. Reading Bennett Cerf, I reverted to being the child who sat under the kitchen table, playing with blocks and listening to his mother talk on the phone. I loved listening to her voice, listening to her half of the conversation and trying to make sense of what she said about people I barely knew and happenings I didn't know at all. I tried to absorb the world through her words and F. W. Dixon's and Bennett Cerf's because eyes merely see things; they cannot connect them, explain them, make sense of them the way words can, even if that understanding is provisional, illusory, wrong.

With time and too much reflection, I also learned from Bennett Cerf's *Laugh Treasury* that a short punchy anecdote could hold complexities beyond the simple turn at the end, and that punch lines, which usually jerk a story to a tidy halt while making the reader smile, could at times deepen the story uncomfortably—like the racism in the Faulkner anecdote— enriching and darkening the emotional shadings of characters they seemed to be flattering. I learned that stories, because they put people in action with other people and the teller in action with his story, are explosive and dangerous organisms that possess a life of their own outside the cage of meaning the teller thinks he has constructed for them. Nowhere was this more true than in church. Whenever the preacher launched into a story, I'd snap out of my stunned daydreaming. I wanted to hear the story no matter what it was, and I was doubly delighted when the story didn't make, or actually undercut, the point the preacher said it made. And from Bennett Cerf not only did I begin to learn how stories were structured because his were stripped to their anecdotal bones, I also grasped that humor was serious. And that pleasure was essential to life and therefore essential to writing—something my Southern Baptist upbringing and my father's stoic Calvinism had hidden from me.

Except for a few of my father's mildewed textbooks from West Point, those are the only books I recall my family owning. At the breakfast table my brother Roger and I squabbled over who got to read the back of the cereal box. When he got up to pour more orange juice, I turned the box of Captain Crunch so I could read it, and when I turned to see if my toast was done he'd shift it back. The squabbling moderated when I was ten or so, and Dad decided I was old enough for him to share sections of the Goldsboro newspaper with me. To his amusement, my favorite section wasn't sports or comics but the editorial page. The news articles merely told me what was happening, but the editorial page revealed ways of thinking about what happened. I was especially drawn to the letters to the editor; from them, I got a clear sense of people who cared passionately about something and had definite opinions about it. Because I knew nothing about the issues being debated, I was of course always utterly convinced by the last letter or editorial I read, a susceptibility that worried me and made me wonder if I were a weak reed in the wind.

Other than the West Point alumni magazine, *Assembly,* and a quarterly publication from the Woodmen of the World, a fraternal insurance company that held my burial insurance policy, the only magazines we subscribed to during my childhood were the *Reader's Digest* and, briefly, *Argosy.* Though I always read the *Reader's Digest,* it didn't interest me very much, except for the jokes, because it lacked personality. A cheap men's magazine that must have been a gift subscription from someone who didn't know my father very well, *Argosy* was not renewed when its year was up. For the year that it came, though, I pored over its true-crime stories and its articles about hunting big game and searching for lost Nazi treasure sunk in Swiss lakes; but what riveted my attention were the corny "lifestyle" pictures—I didn't know they were corny—of bikini-clad babes leaning against the rails of enormous yachts, their hair trailing out over the ocean, their moist lips parted. Though tame even by the standards of the day, the pictures exposed more female flesh than I had ever seen, and I studied them for inspiration and guiltily masturbated over them and then over my memories of them well after the subscription had run out and the old copies were thrown away.

But in the ninth grade I discovered a magazine that changed my life. In the Quonset hut that served as the post newsstand at Camp DeLoges, near Paris, France, I discovered *Time* magazine. Somehow I had made it to fourteen without learning *Time* magazine existed. Here was a world even larger than Bennett Cerf's, to which it bore more than a few affinities with its short takes, celebrity anecdotes, and snappy writing. I loved those famous *Time* magazine VIVID VERBS that never reduced fighter aircraft to doing anything so mundane as "taking off"; they always "scrambled." Stunned and awed by that word choice—and many others—I was positive I would never be able to come up with anything half so colorful. Even more than the clever writing, I loved the sense of a larger world opening beyond the fictional world I loved. But this one was real and it was happening now. *Time* told me about people, places, and things I'd never heard of, and made them all seem comprehensible to a fourteen-year-old boy with little sense of the world outside of family, school, bad books, and the Bible. Except for my age, I must have been one of the provincial but curious readers that Henry Luce fantasized about in his happiest moments.

After my father was transferred from Paris to Montgomery, Alabama—back to the Land of the Round Doorknobs, as Mom called the States—I pestered my parents to buy me a *Time* magazine every time they went near the PX or commissary. And, no, a *Newsweek* or *U.S. News* wouldn't do. I was so insistent, so relentless that they found it easier to subscribe and they kept the subscription until I left the house to get married.

Time covered politics, movies, science, and contemporary culture with more authority, sweep, and style than the local newspapers could muster, and then it covered literary books, even poetry. In each issue, *Time* printed a list of the top ten bestsellers in both fiction and nonfiction, and with an adolescent's uneducated and democratic conviction that what sells best must be the best, I clipped out the lists every week, taped them to three-by-five cards, and filed them in a recipe box my mother had discarded.

While waiting for the best-sellers to come out in paperback, I'd go to the library and read the early works of James Michener, Leon Uris, Saul Bellow, J. D. Salinger, and Mary Renault. It never occurred to me to put my name on the library's waiting list, which I assumed would be two years long and restricted to adults anyway. In Montgomery then there was only one serious bookstore, *Capitol Book and News,* and it was downtown, where my mother seldom went. I'd eagerly go shopping with her so, while she shopped, I could haunt the paperback racks at Woolco, Gaylords, or Bellas Hess, scouring them to see if Michener's *The Source* or some other longed-for book was there. If it was, I'd beg Mom to buy it for me, and though she'd examine it dubiously and grumble about the price or extract a promise to mow the lawn without whining about it, she'd usually pony up for the book. As soon as I began to make a little money by doing yard work for the neighbors, the quarters and much-folded and unfolded dollar bills soon disappeared into cash registers at Gaylords or Bellas Hess, and ultimately, by a process I would not imagine, a portion of it made its way into the hands of Michener, Uris, or Barbara Tuchman, a thought that pleased me.

In the room I shared with my brother Roger I had a closet to myself. And at the back of the overhead shelf I contrived, out of scrap lumber, a series of paperback-sized shelves held in place by the weight of the books. It was precarious and occasionally one end of it would tilt, usually in the middle of the night, noisily dumping the books in a rude jumble. But the house was rented, and Mom wouldn't let me hammer nails into the wall. With the closet door open, I'd lie on my bed and admire the two or three rows of books I'd acquired. I read most of Uris, Michener, and Kurt Vonnegut, and struggled through Swanberg's *Citizen Hearst* and *Theodore Drieser* and Tuchman's *The Proud Tower* and *The Guns of August.* In the books, I kept an index card that doubled as a bookmark, and on it I'd jot down words I didn't know, look them up later, and quiz myself on them to improve my vocabulary. Every month, I'd take the *Reader's Digest* vocabulary test called "It Pays to Increase Your Word Power"; then I'd tear the page out of the magazine and save it so I could work on the words I missed. Every now and then, while looking something up or checking a fact, I'll find one of those index cards or folded *Reader's Digest* pages tucked in an old book, and it's gratifying and reassuring to see that I'm now comfortable with the words that seemed foreign and cumbersome when I was fifteen. With Barbara Tuchman, my list grew so formidable so quickly I had to suspend it until I finished the book, but from her I learned "ancillary." When I used it in an assignment I wrote for eleventh-grade English at Sidney Lanier High, Mrs. Schmidt half-accused me of plagiarism because she, I suspect, didn't know the word before she looked it up in order to question me about it. I was such a mediocre student that I sympathize with her doubting my honesty. I was perversely pleased that she thought my writing was good enough to have been someone else's and I'm still nastily gratified when, looking back, I realize that she didn't seem perturbed, or even to notice, that I pronounced the word "an-Sill-a-ree."

After a year at the Air War College at Maxwell AFB near Montgomery, my father was sent to Cam Ranh Bay in Vietnam while my mother, three brothers, and I stayed put in the rented house on National Avenue. A year later when Dad was restationed at Maxwell, he bought, on North Colonial Avenue, the first house he owned. And it's the house I lived in my senior year of high school, the four years of college, and for the seven months after graduation before I got married. Once I could drive, I'd go to the downtown library or even to the huge Air War College Library out at Maxwell. I rummaged through *Publisher's Weekly* and bound back issues of *Time* and, paying special attention to the old best-seller lists, I couldn't help noticing how regularly *Folk Medicine* by a Dr. Jarvis was listed. One of the huge best-sellers of the late fifties and early sixties, it advocated natural down-home remedies as good for what ails you, whatever that ailment may be. His panacea was, if I'm remembering correctly, eight glasses of water a day, plus two more glasses of water with raw honey and cider vinegar stirred into them. It tasted like weak apple cider gone funky.

My mother was amused by my sudden interest in folk medicine, especially since the eight glasses of water made me, at a hundred and twenty pounds, pee every twenty minutes, and the honey and vinegar concoction made me fart a lot. Though amused, she was also, I think, concerned that I might embrace health-food faddism, a concern I fostered when I announced, "I want to be a vegetarian."

She looked up from the sink, where she was peeling potatoes, and said, "No, you don't." She lapsed into an edgy silence that meant I was going to cause a major battle to erupt if I pushed any further.

Surprised, I thought about it for a minute and realized she was right. I didn't. I really liked meat. But I also realized I didn't want to fight her and my father over meat versus vegetables. They'd grown up poor in rural Georgia during the worst of the Great Depression, and it was important to them that, when we sat down at the supper table, a piece of meat, preferably red meat, be sitting on the table. Chicken was okay, but it wasn't as good as pork and pork wasn't as good as beef. Fish, usually in the form of tuna casserole, salmon croquettes, and fish sticks, was always apologized for—a budget extender. Red meat meant you'd made it. It meant you weren't in red-clay Georgia scuffling to put something, anything, on the table. She let me drink my honey-and-vinegar water, but she wasn't going to compromise on meat just because I'd read something in some book. From time to time, puzzled about my constant reading, she'd ask—occasionally teasing, occasionally serious—"Why do you spend all that time reading things that never really happened? Why do you read about things that aren't true?"

By that time, high school and college, I'd given up trying to explain why I compulsively disappeared into those huge best-sellers. When I didn't know it myself and wouldn't have believed it if someone told me, I couldn't tell my mother that with each book I read—and, by reading, merged with—I was changing who I was. Changing who I was, finding out who I could be: then they were the same thing and perhaps they always are. Almost certainly I could have found out more and changed faster if I'd read better books. On my bed, my back turned to my brother's side of the room, I read, not the classics, which I stubbornly avoided out of a silly sense that classic meant dull and out of a perverse unwillingness to read books that my teachers would approve of, but *Hawaii, Mila 18, Tai Pan, Anthony Adverse, Scaramouche,* and *Catch-22*—as well as *The Carpetbaggers, The Adventurers,* and *Valley of the Dolls.*

In junior high in Paris, I briefly overcame my lazy and falsely democratic aversion to the classics and began reading *War and Peace* because an older boy, another military brat home for Christmas from his sophomore year at Yale, had answered my question about what the greatest novel in the world was by saying that, well, on consideration, he thought *War and Peace* was the greatest novel though he himself would not go so far as to declare Tolstoy the greatest novelist—if I could follow the distinction he was drawing. Dutifully, I went to the school library and checked out *War and Peace*. I could evade Brontë and Dickens, except for a close reading of the Classics Comics version of *A Tale of Two Cities,* but even I could not slip the obligation to read the greatest novel ever written. Besides, I felt outrageously virtuous, mature, adventurous, and almost cool lugging around that great doorstop and foot-crusher of a novel, which in study hall I opened on my desk and read ostentatiously. Though Tolstoy moved with considerably less alacrity than Alfred Payson Terhune's novels about dogs or *The Green Berets,* and though I found the welter of shifting Russian names difficult to organize in my mind, I loved the richly nuanced and complex vision of the world that Tolstoy created. I was transported.

That afternoon my mother asked her usual question, "What happened at school today?" Instead of replying "nothing," the usual answer, I told her that in *War and Peace* I'd read about an elaborate, fancy-dress ball and though I knew I'd merely read it, when I thought back over my day I couldn't shake the feeling I'd actually been at the great and opulent ball in Moscow. I felt that I'd been there, dancing, living those lives I'd read about.

Mom paused, and I knew from the time she was taking to respond that she was thinking, that she was being very careful with me because she didn't know what I was talking about. She may even have been a bit concerned that I was delusional but, no, she told herself, you don't want to overreact. Boys at this age are impressionable, inclined to enthusiasm. I'd better keep an eye on him.

She said, "That's nice, I'm glad you're enjoying your book."

And suddenly I was embarrassed for myself and Tolstoy, for the book he'd written and for my failing to understand that the book was an intimacy between him and me and that I could not expect anyone else to share it. I felt as if I'd blabbed to my mother about one of the oblivious and disdainful schoolgirls I had a crush on, and watched secretly and hungrily and with immense self-loathing. But Tolstoy, in a way they never would or could, had shared his intimacy with me, and I'd betrayed him. To this day, I've never read another word of *War and Peace,* though I've read and admired other works by Tolstoy, and I resolved I'd never again talk to my mother about my reading except in the vaguest terms.

When I went off to college, I didn't go far. Huntingdon College, a small Methodist school, was even closer to my parents' house than Sidney Lanier High. I lived at home, took classes in the morning, worked in the afternoon, and studied—to the extent I studied at all—in the evenings, a schedule that made Huntingdon seem more like thirteenth through sixteenth grade than college. I wish I could blame my after-school jobs for my acceptable but undistinguished record at Huntingdon, but I can't. Other than my laziness and my inability to concentrate on things that don't interest me, I'll blame my reading for some of it. I continued to give my freshest and most engaged attention to reading what I wanted, while working my class assignments into the gaps. I went off on odd reading jags—reading every major Herman Hesse novel, well after the Hesse vogue of a few years earlier had been spent, though I didn't understand the books and could barely follow the plots. Even harder for me to comprehend is my doggedly plowing through every single Evelyn Waugh novel. After I'd read a couple of them, it began to dawn on me that Waugh was not a woman, as I'd supposed, but a man. Though I found the novels easy enough to understand on the surface, I had no way to grasp their tone or intention. Since the copy on the back cover of the paperbacks described some of them as "satirical," I had a vague sense they were supposed to be funny and I read at them almost frantically, thinking that sooner or later the humor would become clear to me and I'd find myself laughing uproariously. It never happened. I also developed a bad habit in college of going to the library or discount store the week before final exams and bringing home eight, nine, ten thrillers and best-sellers, and immersing myself in them with the single-minded concentration that derives from shirking responsibility. In other words, I used books as tranquilizers, a purpose they served, and from time to time continue to serve, admirably.

Huntingdon was a very small college. In my graduating class there were slightly more than a hundred people. Because course offerings were limited, I to my great good fortune was not able to load up on courses in twentieth-century literature and avoid earlier periods the way many students do now at larger schools—and the way I might well have done if I'd had a choice. With so few courses being offered, I either had to take eighteenth-century poetry, say, or nothing; and as it turned out I avoided the twentieth century because I was uncomfortable with Mrs. Stone, who taught those classes. Mrs. Stone—widow of Phil Stone, the man to whom Faulkner dedicated the Snopes trilogy—was a seventy-year-old chain smoker who wore black vinyl go-go boots, and her loud and irritable cynicism coexisted disconcertingly with her Gurdjieffian-cum-Jungian-cum-Episcopalian religious beliefs. Once a year in Delchamps Student Center, Mrs. Stone would, while smoking, show an ancient black-and-white PBS documentary film on Faulkner. Between drags and coughs she'd grouchily answer questions about "Bill," though no one ever had the temerity to ask if she'd had an affair with him, as rumor, born of wishful romanticism, claimed.

I liked being forced to take classes that I'd never have chosen to take. I liked being forced to read closely works I'd never have read on my own—Pope, Dryden, Milton, Shakespeare. I'd assumed they were beyond me. Beyond my ability to comprehend. Beyond even my ability to read. I'd assumed obscurely that they were for students who went to Yale while best-sellers were for people like me. Much of my deep sense of inferiority was personal of course, but a lot of it was Southern, growing out of the cultural stereotypes of the South as peopled by inbred violent dolts who were herded through substandard schools that mistaught us just enough chemistry that we could set up jerry-rigged stills by the chicken house and kill ourselves with lead poisoning—an image that was happily promoted on TV and movies, and in the best-sellers I read so assiduously.

Huntingdon took an avid but uneducated and unformed reader, and gave me Pope, Dryden, Whitman, Fitzgerald, and Shakespeare. I loved the Renaissance classes I took with Mrs. Bell, the folklore with Mrs. Figh, the American lit with Dr. Anderson. I even loved the grammar class with Mrs. Chappell, which was "strongly advised" for those of us, like me, who were earning teaching certificates; and, dear god, I even loved the eighteenth-century English lit course with depressed Dr. Hull, who began every class by complaining about the weather, which was always too hot, too cold, too damp, or too dry for his taste. Then he discussed how bad the economy was and how unlikely it was that any of us would ever be able to get jobs anywhere. From the economy, he would move on to whatever gothic criminal case or filthy political incident was in the local news, and only reluctantly and with great weariness would he pick up his textbook, flip through it, and say with a sigh, "Well, I know y'all don't want to but I guess we'd better talk about this Dryden." Dr. Hull was so unimpressed with my gifts for literary analysis—or so pessimistic about the economy—that when I later asked for a letter of recommendation to graduate school, he tried, in all kindness, to talk me into applying to business school and, after agreeing to write the letter, he sent me away clutching a flyer for an MBA program for humanities students at the University of Virginia.

Even less impressed was Dr. Ellison, the department chairman. Discussing the intellectual abilities of the students with another teacher, she once said pointedly, "Andrew seems like a nice boy." Rather than resent her opinion, I was pleased she thought even that highly of me. In her honors freshman English class, I'd certainly done nothing to impress her. Until she taught me, I had little sense of how to think about literature and no sense of how to organize those thoughts on the page. On more than one occasion Dr. Ellison told me quite pleasantly, as a point of information, that my being permitted to take the honors class had been a misjudgment on her part. I suspect she was trying to fire my competitive instincts. If so, she failed because her assessment of me too closely accorded with my own. All the other students earned an A in the class; I received—and earned—a C. Though patronizing to those like me who deserved it, Dr. Ellison was a brilliant, demanding teacher. She required freshmen to read books as complex as *Light in August, Crime and Punishment,* and *Steppenwolf,* and what she taught me about how to write clearly and think carefully I'd long needed to know.

While I was working on an English major on the second floor of Flowers Hall, down in the basement I was also pursuing a sort of walk-through history major. Truth be told, I was majoring in

Dr. Gordon Chappell, whose classes in American history I took for every single history credit I earned except for one required class in European history and another in political science. A dapper, Vanderbilt-trained historian with a pencil-thin moustache and silver hair parted just off center, Dr. Chappell was a wonderfully acerbic lecturer in the old high style of Southern Tory historians, and I loved to sit in his classes, rapidly scribbling notes from the lectures he delivered from detailed, ancient, and yellowed notes that hadn't changed more than a jot or tittle in thirty years. Though I never read the textbooks, which were boring and would've taken time from my personal reading and my English classes, Dr. Chappell also required us to read four books a semester from a list he provided, and he personally grilled us on each book to make sure we read it. Quickly learning that the biographies were the best written and easiest reading—History Lite—I grew interested in biography as a form in its own right and, over time, biographies have become my preferred light reading, all but displacing thrillers and best-sellers. Two of the books I've written grew out of my fascination with the human life as a measure of, or a way to organize, time. *After the Lost War* is a historical novel in verse that masquerades as a biography of the Civil War veteran and poet Sidney Lanier, and *The Glass Hammer* is an autobiography in verse.

My parents were concerned about my majoring in English and history, and about my wanting to write, especially about my wanting to write poetry. They never tried to talk me out of it, but they worried about money. "How are you going to get a job?" they asked. "How are you going to put meat on the table? What can an English major do that anybody'll pay money for?" Every time we washed the car or did yard work together, my father urged me to study computers. "That's the coming thing," he said, advice I ignored. He grappled with the problem of what kind of job would be suitable for a boy who wanted to do little but read, and my freshman year in college he took a stab at opening my eyes to career opportunities in library science. Escorted by my father, I wound my way around the stacks of the Air War College Library at Maxwell AFB to the book-lined office of the senior librarian, who had, my father intimated, a very high general service rating and consequently quite a nice salary. The senior librarian pumped my hand and clapped me on the shoulder. "Interested in library work, huh?"

"Yes sir," I said. He motioned me to a chair, and I sat uncomfortably while he, equally uncomfortable, extolled the infinite varieties of library work in which one could specialize. My eyes wandered, and I saw that the books lining the book-lined walls weren't books anyone could read; they were technical books about library science, all of them—a revelation that dropped me into a horrified boredom so profound I could barely feign interest in what the senior librarian was saying. Once or twice I forced myself to ask a question because my father was watching me anxiously while pretending not to, hoping something would spark his lethargic son into planning for his future. At home I'd made a little shrine out of the pressed-wood-and-veneer bookshelf my parents had recently bought me, fronting the books up neatly, keeping them in strict order by subject, covering the top shelf with a length of green felt, and lining up my favorite books on top of it—acts of reverence that my parents must have decided, not incorrectly, were the mark of a librarian. But as the senior librarian talked, I realized I was interested only in what was in the books; I had no desire to become a servant to the physical artifact. The idea of spending my life serving the public by looking up Jell-O salad recipes or researching the engine options originally available on 1953 midsized Chevrolet sedans made suicide or teaching school seem like attractive alternatives. And so, as a concession to my parents and to my own fears about finding work, while at Huntingdon I earned a teaching certificate.

In addition to the various day jobs I held in college, I found, in my freshman year, a night job that I held for the next five years. For five dollars a night, I spent four nights a week sleeping in the house of a retired opera singer named Frederick Gunster, whose family was worried about his being alone all night. I'd arrive before 10:00, help Mr. Gunster to bed at 10:30, then check on him before I left in the morning. Later, when he became bedridden, I emptied his hand-held urinal before he went to sleep. If the pay was low, so were the demands on my time and energy, and after I turned out Mr. Gunster's light and shut his bedroom door, I'd rifle his refrigerator, rummage through his liquor cabinet, occasionally taking nips of drinks that were exotic to a boy still living in a house where liquor was disapproved of. My father was a teetotaler but, to his grumbling unhappiness if he stayed up late enough to see it, my mother would mix a very diluted scotch and water, and drink it from a small thick glass that had originally held a frozen shrimp cocktail. But Mr. Gunster possessed something more exotic and fascinating to me than booze. He subscribed to the *New Yorker*, a magazine I'd read about but never seen, and I'd vaguely assumed it no longer existed, like the *Smart Set* and the *American Mercury*. I'd sit up late in his office, playing the *Tonight Show* with the sound turned off on his old black-and-white TV and poring through the articles, stories, cartoons, and studying the poems. Huntingdon then offered no courses in contemporary literature or creative writing, and the small college library carried few literary journals besides *Poetry*, so I was thrilled to read stories by Cheever and Updike and poems by W. S. Merwin, James Dickey, James Wright, Anne Sexton, and Robert Lowell before they appeared in books. At Mr. Gunster's large mahogany desk, I copied poems from the *New Yorker* into notebooks I filled, trying desperately if desultorily to learn how poems worked. I reasoned that copying would focus my attention on rhythm, line breaks, assonance, imagery, and the unfolding structure of the poem, but more than anything else I had a magical belief that I could learn the poems by reading them out loud to make my lips move the way the author's lips had moved and by copying them to make my fingers move the way the author's fingers had moved. Merwin, Dickey, Wright, Sexton, Lowell: I tried to absorb them through my skin.

I've never been entirely sure why I wanted to be a poet. Unlike, I suppose, most poets, my first love in reading was prose—novels first, then nonfiction. But the first time that words jolted my nervous system from head to toe and left it jangling for weeks afterward was in the tenth grade when I flipped ahead in the English textbook to the part we never got to in any English or history class, the part about the twentieth century, and I read T. S. Eliot's "The Hollow Men." I was transported in a way I had never been before and have seldom been since. A certain kind of self-conscious self-pity is woven into the rhythms of both "The Hollow Men" and "The Love Song of J. Alfred Prufrock," a rhythm that adolescents can bond to on a subatomic level even without grasping the surface meaning. I did. With some embarrassment I remember announcing to Dr. Ellison during my freshman year at Huntingdon that it was perfectly possible to understand *The Waste Land* without understanding it on a conscious level. No, she said. One had to be familiar with the allusions, at the very least, before one could claim to understand the poem. Then suddenly she stopped and, to my astonishment, conceded the point. I loved Eliot's poetry before I could understand it, and though I now have the predictable personal and scholarly reservations about the very qualities that first drew me to "The Hollow Men" and "Prufrock," my love for Eliot's poems has stood up through a quarter of a century of close study and continual reading. It's even withstood the fact that I read Evelyn Waugh because he'd taken the title of *A Handful of Dust* from Eliot and I read Hesse because the paperback of *Magister Ludi,* one of the most stupefying novels I've ever staggered to the last page of, had a glowing comment by Eliot splashed across the back cover. Though I don't plan it, at least once a year I read *The Waste Land* and *The Four Quartets* out loud, and I've never made it through *The Four Quartets* without crying.

I was drawn to the intensity of poetry, how concentrated it was, how much meaning, ambiguity, and emotional force it could pack in an image. I loved the intricacies of language and complexities of tone, and most of all I loved the rhythms that carried everything else along on their flood and worked on my nervous system with an immediacy that circumvented thought, and subverted it in ways that were amazing to think of. On another level entirely, I've often wondered if poems weren't the perfect things for a nervous boy with a short but intense attention span to read and write. A boy who couldn't sit at a desk for twenty minutes without blasting from his chair as if by a sudden involuntary contraction of his muscles—a boy who, when he tried to write a short story, would forget by page 12 what color his main character's eyes had been on page 3 and, when he could remember, didn't particularly care.

The hours I spent scouring the *New Yorker* and *Poetry* and then copying poems into my notebooks were nothing compared to the hours I spent every day writing my own bad poems and rewriting them over and over, trying to teach myself to write. I've never understood the contemporary anguish over people having or not having good "role models." To me, one of the things that made writing poetry exciting, made it possible, made it mine was that nobody I knew, including my teachers, did it or knew a damn thing about it, and while I imagine I would've been a better poet sooner if I'd had a good teacher, I also suspect I'd have given it up and found something I could do on my own. The hours I poured into writing and reading contributed to my undistinguished academic record at Huntingdon, of course; but I had a plan. The astonishing number of hours I'd spent writing would come to fruition and I'd be redeemed in the eyes of my teachers, envious friends, and uncomprehending but proud parents when I was accepted into the Writer's Workshop at the University of Iowa, which I naively thought offered a shortcut to literary attainment.

After graduation, I taught elementary school in Montgomery for a year so I could afford to get married, and then I applied to Iowa. I got turned down flat. Though I was crushed and inconsolable, I finally pulled myself together enough to apply to the University of Alabama, where I was accepted late and given a teaching assistantship. The biggest disappointment often opens an unseen door, and the rejection by Iowa turned out to be one of the best things that ever happened to me, despite my resentful and obstinate refusal for a long time to acknowledge that fact. For the first time I understood no deus ex machina was going to save me, solve my future, justify my life. I couldn't count on shortcuts or early success to lessen the uncertainty of struggling to write well. In addition to working hard, I was going to have to learn to *think* about what I read. Thought, though an essential part of the aesthetic experience, is for me a secondary response to putting on the author's nervous system and feeling the world through his fingertips and thinking with her thoughts. As a child, I simply surrendered myself to the book I was reading, accepted its premises without question, and lived in its world on its terms. When I had to leave, booted out by the turning of the last page, I dropped into a slight depression, a short period of grieving, if you will, that I still experience when I come to the end of a book that has swept me beyond the resistance of my own logic and personality, and now returns me to them. And I must wait a decent interval, a couple of hours or a day, before I jump into another book, or I feel like a widower who remarries with unseemly haste, standing at the altar saying "I do" with the dirt of his first wife's grave still on his shoes.

So I resisted literary analysis, afraid it would hinder my ability to enter completely into that world. And for bad writing, it has. Good writing, powerful imagining, can still overwhelm all the defenses of an intellect that welcomes joyfully its own invasion. Though I committed myself only late and reluctantly to the disciplines of thought, at Alabama and later at Syracuse University I worked as hard as I physically could to become a serious student of literature, a good reader, a voluptuary of enduring pleasures. And when at thirty, after the breakup of my marriage, I was accepted by the Writer's Workshop, which offered me, at the price of only minimal poverty, two years to do nothing but read and write, I turned down a good job, stored thirty-five boxes of books in my father's utility shed, and I went.

II

Essays

"A Monument of Labor Lost": The Sonnets of Frederick Goddard Tuckerman

I first became aware of the poetry of Frederick Goddard Tuckerman when I was putting together a syllabus for a sophomore American literature survey. Flipping through a table of contents to get page numbers, I noticed Tuckerman's name and thought, "Who the hell is that! I've never heard of *him* before." (As it turns out I was mistaken even about my own ignorance. Edmund Wilson mentions Tuckerman and quotes a couple of his sonnets in *Patriotic Gore*—a discussion I'd breezed through several years before.) There were only eight pages of his poetry in the anthology, so, out of curiosity, I tossed Tuckerman's name on the syllabus, figuring I'd learn something when the time came to prepare for class. I did. I discovered a compelling, occasionally powerful, and often ragged poet who seems to me the major poetic link between nineteenth-century British poetry and the American poetry of the early twentieth century—a poet who astounds me with his strikingly modern imagery and who makes me agonize for him as he seeks, sometimes successfully, to speak a distinctly modern American poetic idiom.

Tuckerman has been rediscovered twice since the second American edition of *Poems,* the only book of his work published in his lifetime. *Poems* first appeared in a private printing in 1860 and last appeared in a commercial edition in America in 1869. The first rediscovery was made by Witter Bynner, who, in 1931,

From *Chicago Review* 37 no. 1 (Winter 1990): 64–79. Reprinted by permission of *Chicago Review.*

edited *The Sonnets of Frederick Goddard Tuckerman,* which led to a small but steady interest in Tuckerman's poetry. That small steady interest peaked thirty-four years later when N. Scott Momaday published *The Collected Poems of Frederick Goddard Tuckerman.* Momaday's editing brought together for the first time Tuckerman's fine sonnet series and his important poem "The Cricket," as well as the generally dismal poems that appeared during Tuckerman's life and earned him the lack of attention they deserve. With the sonnets and "The Cricket" shrewdly loaded at the front of the book, Momaday's edition received some attention from reviewers and critics, and resulted in Tuckerman's finding a place in several prominent anthologies, including *The Norton Anthology of Poetry* and Macmillan's *Anthology of American Literature,* in which I chanced upon the poems. But now he is starting to slide out of the more recent anthologies and new editions of established anthologies. Tuckerman's "Fifth Series" of sonnets ends with this modest prayer that I would like to echo for him as he seems poised to slip back into unmerited obscurity:

> Let me give something!—As the years unfold,
> Some faint fruition though not much, my most:
> Perhaps a monument of labor lost.
> But thou, who givest all things, give not me
> To sink in silence.[1]

Over and above its own considerable artistry, the poetry of Frederick Goddard Tuckerman is remarkable for the other voices it contains. Within Tuckerman's poems one hears Shakespeare, Keats, Wordsworth, and Tennyson very clearly. More— and better—than any other American poet of his age, Tuckerman strove to take the British voices and cadences of what Matthew Arnold called the "grand style" and adapt them to the American tongue. The results are mixed. Sometimes the voices remain unassimilated. But on occasion, something truly remarkable, truly prescient, happens. The contemporary reader hears faintly, but clearly, voices that Tuckerman could not have heard and from poets who most likely had not read Tuckerman.

Irving Howe sees adumbrations of E. A. Robinson in these lines from "The Stranger," though he qualifies the comparison by noting that the lines lack "Robinson's genius for psychological penetration":[2]

> Where silence brooded, I longed to look within
> On the completed story of his life
> So easy still it seemed to lift the hand,
> And open it, as I would a disused door
> Locked with a dusty web: but he passed out;
> And if he had a grief it went with him,
> And all the treasure of his untold love.

(118)

Howe is not the only astute reader to hear pre-echoes of Robinson in Tuckerman's work. In sonnet 5 of the "First Series," Edwin Cady hears Santayana, Robinson, and "even Eliot":[3]

> And so the day drops by, the horizon draws
> The fading sun and we stand struck in grief,
> Failing to find our haven of relief,
> Wide of the way, nor sure to turn or pause,
> And weep to view how fast the splendor wanes
> And scarcely heed that yet some share remains
> Of the red afterlight, some time to mark,
> Some space between the sundown and the dark;
> But not for him those golden calms succeed
> Who while the day is high and glory reigns
> Sees it go by, as the dim pampas plain,
> Hoary with salt and gray with bitter weed,
> Sees the vault blacken, feels the dark wind strain,
> Hears the dry thunder roll, and knows no rain.

(5)

After the workmanlike opening ten lines—fine, but undistinguished—the last four lines amaze us, both by the sinewy power of their own expression and by how clearly they anticipate the themes and imagery of *The Waste Land*. And "imagery" in the twentieth-century use of the word seems utterly appropriate in discussing these sonnets because Tuckerman frequently employs the twentieth-century poet's painstakingly learned technique of ending the poem with a striking image that gives a powerful sense of closure while at the same time opening the poem up to larger and more ambivalent resonances.

The remarkable adumbrations continue. Consider the first sonnet of the "Second Series." The poem delicately evokes Keats's "To Autumn" while it ends up sounding like no one else so much as Robert Frost:

> That boy, the farmer said, with hazel wand
> Pointing him out, half by the haycock hid,
> Though bare sixteen, can work at what he's bid
> From sun till set, to cradle, reap, or band.
> I heard the words, but scarce could understand
> Whether they claimed a smile or gave me pain:
> Or was it aught to me, in that green lane,
> That all day yesterday, the briars amid,
> He held the plough against the jarring land
> Steady, or kept his place among the mowers
> Whilst other fingers, sweeping for the flowers,
> Brought from the forest back a crimson stain?
> Was it a thorn that touched the flesh, or did
> The pokeberry spit purple on my hand?

(19)

The lightly evoked Yankee dialect of the farmer, the personal ambivalence of the speaker, the careful irony of the rhetorical questions, and the assured "sound of sense" as the discourse plays through the meter, line breaks, and imagery all remind me so much of Frost that I can hardly credit that the author never had the opportunity to study Frost and deliberately imitate him. On closer inspection, though, differences emerge other than the inevitable, if surprisingly few, archaisms: the occasional inversion of colloquial speech order ("the briars amid"); the slightly splashy imagery and the passionate alliteration of the last line; and the guilt that comes from the speaker's not working while others do. Compared to Frost, Tuckerman's sonnet is less sly, more earnest.

To move even closer to the present, the end of sonnet 6 of the "Second Series"—to choose just one example—reminds me of Robert Lowell with its violent intellectual imagery. "Perfect grief, like love," the poet says, "should cast out fear"; it avoids "ignorant praise" as well as those who "pick with sharpened fingers for a flaw":

> Better than this were surgery rough as that
> Which, hammer and chisel in hand, at one sharp blow
> Strikes out the wild tooth from a horse's jaw.
>
> (21)

Perhaps I'm going too far when I see Roethke's "Flower Dump" or "The Geranium" presaged in sonnet 5 of the "Second Series." As ardent naturalists they both probably saw similar sights and were struck by their metaphorical and metaphysical possibilities. In Tuckerman's poem, the man who loves nature finds that "his thought stands like the things he loves." So far, so Emersonian. But Tuckerman apparently had friends who were more cynical than the people with whom Emerson talked. Still, he remains hopeful, if not confident, that his ideas, which they now discard, will later take root and bloom:

> The friend may listen with a sneering cheek,
> Concede the matter good and wish good luck,
> Or plainly say, "Your brain is planet-struck!"
> And drop your hoarded thought as vague and vain
> Like bypast flowers, to redden again in rain,
> Flung to the offal heap with shard and shuck.
>
> (21)

While both poets' loving concern for flowers leads them to the same image, it seems to me that Tuckerman handles it better than Roethke, whose "Flower Dump" ends with one romantic tulip atop the heap of limp flowers. Tuckerman seizes more fully on the possibilities of the image; he explores its implications more and establishes it more realistically in a larger perspective.

Probably the most remarkable of Tuckerman's sonnets and certainly the best known, in the small world of Tuckerman aficionados, is sonnet 10 of the "First Series." In some of the sonnets I've quoted, there is the fascinating sense of imagery and metaphor teetering on the edge of becoming symbolism—and this in rural Massachusetts by a man who died in 1873. One is almost reminded of Ezra Pound's writing incredulously to Harriet Monroe about the young T. S. Eliot: "He has actually trained *and* modernized himself *on his own*." Almost. Here is the poem that Eugene England in a provocative and intelligent essay calls "the first post-symbolist poem":[4]

> An upper chamber in a darkened house,
> Where, ere his footsteps reached ripe manhood's brink,
> Terror and anguish were his cup to drink;
> I cannot rid the thought nor hold it close
> But dimly dream upon the man alone:
> Now though the autumn clouds most softly pass,
> The cricket chides beneath the doorstep stone
> And greener than the season grows the grass.
> Nor can I drop my lids nor shade my brows,
> But there he stands beside the lifted sash;
> And with a swooning of the heart, I think
> Where the black shingles slope to meet the boughs
> And, shattered on the roof like smallest snows,
> The tiny petals of the mountain ash.
>
> (7)

In its subtle use of natural imagery to express feelings that border on or merge into the ineffable, this superb poem reminds me of Pound's *Cathay* poems. Eugene England argues, convincingly to my mind, that the speaker of the poem is the older Tuckerman, in autumn, remembering his younger self looking out the window in spring, when the petals of the mountain ash fall.[5] As they fall, they summon to mind the snow that is to come. England also suggests that the upper chamber, with its allusion to Christ's Last Supper, is in actuality the room in which Tuckerman's beloved wife Anna died in 1857. Reading through *Personae*, it is easy to see Pound struggle through his love for the romantic excesses and gestures of language to his mature style. Tuckerman could never entirely make the change. Even his best poems are marred, as England points out, by twisted diction and archaic phrasing ("ere his footsteps reached ripe manhood's brink"), and a reliance on romantic clichés to pad out the line, or worse, to make crucial emotional transitions in the poem ("and with a swooning of the heart"). But these flaws only marginally detract from the sheer brilliance and power of sonnet 10, which I think is not only Tuckerman's best poem but also one of the best American poems written in the nineteenth century.

Why, then, has Tuckerman not received the acclaim he deserves? In his own time, his comparatively rough meters were probably considered unpleasing at best and inept at worst. The same is true for his loose rhyming; occasionally lines end with words that don't have a rhyme at all. Now, however, these traits are an accepted practice. They are even harmonious to the contemporary ear, which tends to be jarred by meter and rhyme that are too insistent. It is our tendency to interpret these types of variation as evidence of the form's collapsing under the pressure of the content. That is, we intuit that what the poet has to say is more important than how he says it, and we perceive that effect, in a good poet, as sincerity, not incompetence—though in a bad poet it can certainly be both. Another reason for his obscurity is that, in Tuckerman's own lifetime, the sonnet was not a popular form. As Samuel Golden points out, the sonnet was suspect as a British import and therefore unsuited to American subjects.[6] Indeed, the sonnet has never been all that popular in America, and the sonnet sequence even less so. And that leads to another reason Tuckerman hasn't found his place in the anthologies. He was not in the thrall of the American love of originality at the expense of all else. He was not specifically engaged in that enterprise beloved of anthologists and scholars: the drive to create a unique American idiom to give expression to uniquely American experiences. Tuckerman's poems are clearly set in New England, and when they are at their best the voice is pretty clearly a New England voice. The poems are American, though not stridently, self-consciously so. But clearly too, Tuckerman's masters were the British poets of the great tradition; and in American poetry, from Walt Whitman through William Carlos Williams and beyond, there has existed an uneasy suspicion of those writers who look to England for their models. Tuckerman's originality was evolutionary, growing indisputably out of the work of his masters as well as out of the world in which he lived. He had no desire to be sui generis.

To be rediscovered, it helps if an author has a special claim on the attention of the reader. If, for instance, Tuckerman were a nineteenth-century Southerner, writing in a time and a region when good poetry was scarce, he might have received more attention than he has because anthologists strive to maintain some sort of geographical balance and because scholars in a region have a natural tendency to promote their own. Thus, more people have heard of and read (and can quote!) the poetry of Sidney Lanier, though Tuckerman is considerably superior to Lanier as a poet. And Tuckerman, born in nineteenth-century Massachusetts, has to compete for attention with the great writers of the New England renaissance as well as with the established but perfectly dreary Fireside Poets, who are always included in anthologies because of their historical importance rather than their artistic merit. Tuckerman has also suffered from the bad timing of the efforts to vivify his reputation. N. Scott Momaday's *The Collected Poems of Frederick Goddard Tuckerman* came out as scholarly concern was shifting toward broadening the canon to include authors excluded because of race, gender, and ethnic origin. As a rich, white male of Anglo-Saxon stock, Tuckerman had no appeal to such scholars. And Witter Bynner's *The Sonnets of Frederick Goddard Tuckerman* came out in the early 1930s when the High Modernists were at their most elevated. But such quirks of time, literary competition, and transitory political considerations aside, the artistry of the work remains and calls for our attention—and rewards the attention we give it.

Where then would I rank Frederick Goddard Tuckerman? One of the worst things that can happen to a poet of modest but important gifts is to be overvalued, because new readers come to the work and are disappointed that it's not as good as they'd been led to expect. I suspect that Tuckerman, though dead ninety years when it was written, has suffered from Yvor Winters's claim in the foreword to *The Collected Poems* that Tuckerman is "one of the three most remarkable poets of the nineteenth century" (ix). The other two are Emily Dickinson and Jones Very, and the inclusion of Very with Tuckerman immediately alerts the reader that Winters is not merely a revisionist but a full-blown crank, though he is often a useful and enlightening crank. Winters goes on to boost Tuckerman by thumping the rest of nineteenth-century American poetry:

Emerson had talent, which was badly damaged by foolish think-
ing; Bryant might be described as a fine second-rate poet, better
than most of the British poets of the century. Of Poe and Whit-
man, the less said the better. (xvi)

He doesn't stop there. By the end of the foreword, Winters has
changed his mind on "The Cricket," Tuckerman's only truly
brilliant poem that's not a sonnet. In an earlier essay, he had
persuasively called it "one of the great meditations on death to
be written since the seventeenth century."[7] Fifteen years later,
he sees things in somewhat more hyperbolic terms: "*The Cricket*, I
feel sure, is the greatest poem in English of the century" (xvi).
"The Cricket" is a good poem. A fine poem. A poem that de-
serves to be in every inclusive anthology of American literature.
It is not, however, better than "Song of Myself," "Ode: Intima-
tions of Immortality," Keats's great odes, or "In Memoriam"—
just to toss off the first exceptions that leap to a mind slightly
numbed by Winters's outlandish claims. But to stop avoiding the
question I've posed for myself, I'd judge Tuckerman's artistic
accomplishment to be less, by a long shot, than that of Whitman
or Dickinson. He's better than all the Fireside Poets. Better than
Oliver Wendell Holmes, Lanier, and even Bryant. To establish a
rough category, I'd say that Tuckerman's poetry is as good as
that of Emerson, Thoreau, Poe, and Melville.

Though offering such judgments is an uncomfortable task, it
is probably unavoidable when you're arguing that more atten-
tion and respect should be given to a neglected poet. Now I want
to return to Tuckerman's poetry and, by way of conclusion, look
at two aspects of it: Tuckerman's attitudes toward nature and the
ways he weaves the sonnets together to make a coherent series of
them and not just a collection of more or less random sonnets.

Tuckerman's best poetry is his nature poetry—and it's some
of the best nature poetry written by an American. It stands out
for a loving attention to the minute and particular that easily
surpasses Emerson and almost rivals the prose of Thoreau.
Tuckerman was a gentleman scientist of the nineteenth-century
sort: a highly trained amateur who chose the avocation for the
love of it. And since he practiced it to the exclusion of the law,
for which he had been formally educated, it's fair to say it was an

avocation that in his commitment and passion bordered on vocation. The critics are divided, however, on Tuckerman's attitude toward nature. Golden says Tuckerman is a Transcendentalist (p. 20); England flatly calls him "singularly anti-romantic"[8]; and Momaday, in his introduction to Tuckerman's *Collected Poems,* traces some of his agreements and disagreements with Emerson before concluding:

> It is against the background of Emersonian Romanticism that Witter Bynner's statement about Tuckerman becomes sharply meaningful. Tuckerman is indeed "isolated in an intense integrity toward nature." Superficially, he preserves the stage properties of Romantic literature: the spirit of isolation, a dissociation of emotional cause and effect, a preoccupation with nature. But Tuckerman's sense of isolation is defined in terms of intellectual honesty rather than self-reliance; his taste is measured in the fact rather than the celebration of sentiment; his attention is trained upon the surfaces rather than the symbols of the world. (xxv–xxvi)

While Momaday is closer to the truth than England or Golden, he's a bit facile when he implies that Tuckerman is honest when he views the surfaces of nature but merely mired in his own time or perhaps even dishonest when he employs "the stage properties of Romantic literature." Certainly Tuckerman is at his worst as a poet when he overindulges his romantic bent. But like, say, Emily Dickinson, Tuckerman was both romantic and antiromantic. His mind was inclined to fly to the heights of romantic excess; his heart was in the mundane, even technical, details of his garden. Tuckerman states the dichotomy quite clearly—and does not attempt to resolve it—in sonnet 7 of the "Second Series," a poem that is as clear an *ars poetica* as we get from him:

> His heart was in his garden; but his brain
> Wandered at will among the fiery stars.
> Bards, heroes, prophets, Homers, Hamilcars,
> With many angels stood, his eye to gain;
> The devils, too, were his familiars:
> And yet the cunning florist held his eyes
> Close to the ground, a tulip bulb his prize,

And talked of tan and bonedust, cutworms, grubs,
As though all Nature held no higher strain;
Or, if he spoke of art, he made the theme
Flow through boxborders, turf, and flower tubs
Or, like a garden engine's, steered the stream,
Now spouted rainbows to the silent skies,
Now kept it flat and raked the walls and shrubs.

(22)

I love this poem: the stately but lively iambic pentameter; the tender regard for the homely that gives us "grubs," "tubs," and "shrubs" as rhymes; and the glorious diminuendo of the last line after the rhetorical crescendo of the line that precedes it. There is, yes, an inclination to choose the antiromantic over the romantic but that choice is called "cunning," in the several senses of that word; and there is a deep yearning after romantic language and the romantic flights of imagination expressed in the first five lines of the poem. At the end of the poem, when Tuckerman finally must choose, he chooses both. At one moment he directs the stream of water romantically upward to "sprout rainbows to the silent skies"; at the next, he directs it to the pedestrian task of cleaning the garden.

The model behind Tuckerman's inability to decide between loving the world for itself or loving it as something to look beyond is probably his beloved Tennyson, specifically the Tennyson of "In Memoriam," which was first published in 1850, four years before Tuckerman began his first two series of sonnets. In 1857, Tuckerman's wife Anna died and her death is at the heart of all the sonnet sequences, almost as deeply as Arthur Hallam's was at the heart of "In Memoriam." Stunned by Hallam's death, Tennyson reaches out to see if he can wrest some consolation from a Christian faith that is powerfully under attack by scientific materialism—and thereby hangs much of the tension of "In Memoriam." In a more muted way, Tuckerman often finds that his skeptical, scientific mind undercuts the impulse toward a form of Transcendentalism that shades into a vague Christianity. Bereft at the loss of his wife he reaches out to the beyond, while at the same time suspecting that this world, as it is, may be the end-all and be-all of life.

The spiraling of thought through Tuckerman's five series of sonnets is less like the plotting of traditional sonnet sequences and more like the obsessive psychological working out of modern poetic sequences like, say, John Berryman's *The Dream Songs*. Tuckerman was, I think, being very precise when he called his larger poetic constructs "series" instead of "sequences." The loosely circling meditations have the ebb and flow of intellect and emotion trying to come to accommodation, if not accord. Sometimes the only connection between one poem and the next is that they are generally on the same subject; at other times there are clear sequences within the larger series, stretches in which the poems clearly move logically from one to the next, developing a thought, wrestling with it, or contradicting it: tight riffs within the looser orchestration of the whole. The immediate model for this type of organization is likely Tennyson's "In Memoriam."

The give and take of the series can be seen at work in the last six sonnets of the "First Series" in which the dialectic of romanticism and antiromanticism, belief and science, emotion and intellect is particularly pronounced. Tuckerman's romanticism is evident in sonnet 23. In this poem, with joy and without any apparent skepticism, he embraces the supernatural claim of a young woman who tells him that she has seen Anna, his deceased wife, return as a ghost. Almost certainly Tuckerman is conjuring up Milton's identically numbered sonnet, the great sonnet that begins "Methought I saw my late espoused saint / Brought to me like *Alcestis* from the grave." Here is Tuckerman's poem:

> Shall I not see her? yes: for one has seen
> Her in her beauty since we called her dead,
> One like herself, a fair young mother led
> By her own lot to feel compassion keen;
> And unto her last night my Anna came
> And sat within her arms and spoke her name
> While the old smile, she said, like starlight gleamed,
> And like herself in fair young bloom she said,
> Only the white more white, the red more red,
> And fainter than the mist her pressure seemed.
> And words there were, though vague yet beautiful,
> Which she who heard them could not tell to me;

> It is enough: my Anna did not flee
> To grief or fear, nor lies in slumber dull.

> (14)

Though hardly Tuckerman at his best, the poem has a graceful opening and some good writing in lines 9 through 13 to compensate partially for the clichés, the lackluster last line, and the rather alarming echoes of Edgar Allan Poe. The way the poem turns on "It is enough" is sad and touching even though tinged with bathos. In the very next poem, however, he begins by challenging his own romantic faith in the supernatural, saying "Perhaps a dream" (14). Immediately, he addresses the issue of the mundane versus the spiritual and comes down, at least for the moment, on the side of the spiritual: "yet surely truth has beamed / Oft from the gate of dreams upon the brain." While the writing here is clumsy, it improves as Tuckerman employs one of the poet's best approaches to a difficult and charged subject about which he has ambivalent feelings: the rhetorical question. The questions allow Tuckerman to pose possible ideas and attitudes without committing himself to them:

> Why do men doubt, and balance, and disdain
> Where she, the gentler spirit, seeks to skim
> Light from the vague, though thick the shadows swim,
> Still counting what she may not all explain—
> Not to be lost, or lightly disesteemed
> Though cloudy of shape it seem, and meaning dim?

> (14)

These are not, it seems to me, merely rhetorical questions. They are real and anguished requests for an answer, as Tuckerman laments his own skepticism, his own inability to let go of his doubts and believe. The poem ends with three more questions, each more troubled and doubting than the one before it, as the skeptic challenges his own skepticism:

> Did Manoah's wife doubt ere she showed to him
> The angel standing in the golden grain?
> Had Deborah fear? or was that vision vain
> That Actia, Arlotte, and Mandane dreamed?

> (14)

Grief-stricken, he falls deeper in doubt. In sonnet 25, he thinks of Anna and remembers "the mountains where our love began" (15). Now, however, he will "pore upon the landscape like a book / But cannot find her." Instead, the remembered landscape remains itself. He imagines the distant events of the Civil War or only the meaningless details of the world:

> there rise to me
> Gardens and groves in light and shadow outspread;
> Or on a headland far away I see
> Men marching slow in orderly review,
> And bayonets flash as, wheeling from the sun,
> Rank after rank give fire: or sad, I look
> On miles of moonlit brine, with many a bed
> Of wave weed heaving. There the wet sands shine
> And just awash, the low reef lifts its line.

(15)

The controlled assonance and alliteration of those last three plaintive lines are nothing short of remarkable.

If the landscape can sometimes be inscrutable, at other times it can be downright deceptive. In sonnet 26, a poem that is about as removed from Emerson as one can get, Tuckerman tells, with becoming and self-mocking humility, about times when he was sure he was reading nature right, only to find out that he was wrong—and that so was nature itself:

> For Nature daily through her grand design
> Breathes contradiction where she seems most clear,
> For I have held of her the gift to hear
> And felt indeed endowed of sense divine
> When I have found by guarded insight fine,
> Cold April flowers in the green end of June,
> And thought myself possessed of Nature's ear
> When by the lovely mill-brook into mine,
> Seated on slab or trunk asunder sawn,
> The night-hawk blew his horn at summer noon;
> And in the rainy midnight I have heard
> The ground sparrow's long twitter from the pine,
> And the catbird's silver song, the wakeful bird
> That to the lighted window sings for dawn.

(15)

This observation about the world is applied to the mind in sonnet 27. The mind, brooding on these peculiarities of nature (and perhaps the mind brooding on itself: the referent to the pronoun in the first line is obscure), comes to see that things are often not what they appear.

> So to the mind long brooding but on it
> A haunting theme for anger, joy, or tears,
> With ardent eyes, not what we think appears;
> But hunted home, behold! its opposite.
>
> (16)

From this opening, the poem veers out into how hope turns to grief and love to woe, and laments how "all human life" is "born into pain and ending bitterly," though there is some hope of transitory happiness in between birth and death:

> Worn sorrow breaking in disastrous mirth,
> And wild tears wept of laughter, like the drops
> Shook by the trampling thunder to the earth;
> And each seems either, or but a counterfeit
> Of that it would dissemble: hopes are fears
> And love is woe: nor here the discord stops;
> But through all human life runs the account,
> Born into pain and ending bitterly—
> Yet sweet perchance, betweentime, like a fount
> That rises salt and freshens to the sea.
>
> (16)

Now that the writer has found both nature and human perceptions of nature to be ultimately flawed, he comes, surprisingly, to the solution of the Puritans: we must turn our backs to the world and seek God. Only He can give meaning to our lives: "Not the round natural world, nor the deep mind, / The reconcilement holds . . . ; / And but in Him may we our import find" (16). Without faith in God, "The agony to know, the grief, the bliss / Of toil, is vain and vain." This sonnet, the final sonnet in the "First Series," ends with imagistic, arbitrary brilliance that brings to mind again the forced concluding sections of "In Memoriam":

No more thy meaning seek, thine anguish plead,
But leaving straining thought and stammering word,
Across the barren azure pass to God:
Shooting the void in silence like a bird,
A bird that shuts his wings for better speed.

(16)

This is self-exhortation. The poet *wills* the emotion in the hope that by saying it he might make it so: it does not have the force of belief behind it. Even as he rejects the natural world, he returns to it for the image of the bird folding its wings to its body to increase its speed. And as much as it becomes a symbol for the human soul seeking God, the lovingly exact observation of the bird remains as testimony to Tuckerman's love of the world and of his not being able to deny it.

At the beginning of this essay, I quoted the first part of Tuckerman's last sonnet, a poem in which he prays that he not be allowed to "sink in silence" even if the result is that his poems stand, as they have for over a century, only as "a monument of labor lost." I am now almost ready to quote the rest of the poem. In *Poetry and the Age,* Randall Jarrell says that "a good poet is someone who manages, in a lifetime of standing out in thunderstorms, to be struck by lightning five or six times; a dozen or two dozen times and he is great."[9] Frederick Goddard Tuckerman was struck, solidly, five or six times by lightning—"struck scarlet," as he says, when at the end of his final sonnet (sonnet 16, "Fifth Series"), he too explores the image of the lightning strike and what it means:

But thou, who givest all things, give not me
To sink in silence, seared with early cold,
Frost-burnt and blackened, but quick fire for frost!
As once I saw at a houseside, a tree
Struck scarlet by the lightning, utterly
To its last limb and twig: so strange it seemed,
I stopped to think if this indeed were May,
And were those wildflowers? or had I dreamed?
But there it stood, close by the cottage eaves,
Red-ripened to the heart: shedding its leaves
And autumn sadness on the dim spring day.

(66)

Let this stand as an image for Frederick Goddard Tuckerman. His art turned death, at least momentarily, into something vivid, vibrant, beautiful, and oddly outside of time. And like the tree, Tuckerman's gifts, at their truest, seem to belong to the imagistic brilliance of a later age, as they blazed almost unseen in the springtime of the American literary renaissance.

NOTES

1. Frederick Goddard Tuckerman, *The Collected Poems of Frederick Goddard Tuckerman,* ed. Scott Momaday (New York, Oxford University Press, 1965), 66. Page citations of all subsequent quotations from this book will be given parenthetically in the text of this essay.

2. Irving Howe, "An American Poet," *New York Review of Books,* 25 March 1965, 18.

3. Edwin Cady, "Frederick Goddard Tuckerman," in *Essays in American Literature in Honor of Jay B. Hubbell,* ed. Clarence Gohdes (Durham: Duke University Press, 1967), 143.

4. Eugene England, "Tuckerman's Sonnet 1:10: The First Post-Symbolist Poem," *Southern Review* 12 (Spring 1976): 323.

5. Ibid., 335–37.

6. Samuel Golden, *Frederick Goddard Tuckerman* (New York: Twayne, 1966), 17.

7. Yvor Winters, "A Discovery," *Hudson Review* 3(Autumn 1950): 458.

8. England, 323

9. Randall Jarrell, *Poetry and the Age* (New York: Farrar, Straus and Giroux, 1953), 148.

"One and Zero Walk Off Together": Galway Kinnell's *The Book of Nightmares*

In *The Book of Nightmares,* Galway Kinnell explores from a contemporary perspective one of the great themes of romantic poetry: What is the proper human response to death? For Kinnell the answer to that question is complicated by his being possessed of a deep spiritual longing while living in an existential world. And death, that ultimate existential fact, is the stumbling block to spiritual aspirations because it implies utter nullity. But even with life ending in the apparent finality of death, people often intuit a harmony beyond death, a unity in the universe. Kinnell, in an interview, has stated this dichotomy succinctly: "death has two aspects—the extinction, which we fear, and the flowing away into the universe, which we desire—there is a conflict within us that I want to deal with."[1] Or to state the proposition in explicitly Freudian terms, people are torn between a drive toward life and a drive toward death. Behind this dualism, however, lies a deeper one; the rational mind looks at the world and sees that life, to all evidence, ends with death, while the irrational mind intuits a mystical oneness in death.

Throughout *The Book of Nightmares* Kinnell struggles to develop a coherent view of life and death, and his examination of his own ambivalences leads him to unravel a string of connected dualities—conscious and unconscious, rational and irrational, mind and body, and ultimately mortality and immortality. Like Carl Jung, Kinnell feels that in the modern world the logical

From *American Poetry* 3 (Fall 1985): 56–71.

mind has grown too powerful at the expense of the unconscious. He therefore exalts the wisdom of the body that taps into the unconscious, but finds the mind often blocks his access to it. All through the volume the poet honestly confronts both sides of the dichotomy, and never slides off into glib lyricism or the intellectual fuzziness of fashionable mysticism.

The book begins with Kinnell, after the birth of his daughter Maud, going out into the woods, where "by this wet site / of old fires," he starts a fire for his daughter.[2] While the fire built on the ashes of an earlier fire hints at immortality through one's offspring, the speaker's main concern is about having brought a life, represented by the fire, into a world hostile to it. In spite of the rain, as an act of affirmation, he is able to start the fire. As the wood burns, the deathwatch beetles inside it "begin running out of time" (3). Relishing the wordplay of *deathwatch*, Kinnell introduces a theme he will return to frequently: In the hour of our birth is the hour of our death. But why? The answer, which he will expand on later, is implicit in his description of what happens when the rain falls on the fire. The fire changes the rain, as people's attitude to their suffering can change it into a means of attaining wisdom:

> The raindrops trying
> to put the fire out
> fall into it and are
> changed: the oath broken,
> the oath sworn between earth and water, flesh and spirit,
>   broken,
> to be sworn again,
> over and over, in the clouds and to be broken again,
> over and over, on earth.
>
> (4)

In transcending earthly suffering and rising into the clouds, flesh and spirit join, but on earth, which is imperfect and subject to mortality, the joining breaks down, resulting in the uneasy division of the human psyche between allegiance to mind and to body. At death, however, one returns to the universe, unity is restored, and the oath is sworn anew.

The harmony to be found in death can also be seen, though it fades rapidly, in newborn children. The poet's thoughts return to his daughter, who was born just hours earlier. Before birth she was whole, "somersaulting alone in the oneness" of the womb (5). Kinnell's description of the child as she is separated from oneness by birth is powerful and moving:

> she skids out on her face into light,
> this peck
> of stunned flesh
> clotted with celestial cheesiness, glowing
> with the astral violet
> of the underlife. And as they cut
>
> her tie to the darkness
> she dies
> a moment, turns blue as a coal,
> the limbs shaking
> as the memories rush out of them.
>
> (6)

The memories of the collective unconscious are lost or made subservient to the rational mind, and the child dies for a moment, suspended between the life of the unconscious and the conscious mind. Once she is born, she is inevitably thrust into the emptiness that follows the loss of the oneness she enjoyed in the womb. While the doctors hold her up by the feet, she draws her first breath, "the slow, / beating, featherless arms / already clutching at the emptiness" (7). Forced out of the harmony and fullness of the womb, she instinctively embraces the emptiness of the existential world.

Later, the poet hears Maud crying in her crib and attributes her crying to "a sadness / stranger than ours, all of it / flowing from the other world" (7). Behind this description and the description of Maud at birth—"clotted with celestial cheesiness, glowing / with the astral violet / of the underlife"—I hear the voice of Wordsworth, another poet who felt intimations of immortality when recollecting early childhood and who described children as born "trailing clouds of glory" that diminish as the conscious mind grows.[3] The longer Maud lives, the more she loses of the dark knowledge of the unconscious from which she came and to which she may return. To provide for Maud when she needs that knowledge and finds herself cut off from it by the blindness of her own rational mind, Kinnell sings to her so that, when the time comes,

> you will remember,
> in the silent zones
> of the brain, a specter, descendant
> of the ghostly forefathers, singing
> to you in the nighttime
>
> (7)

The song she will hear is not the bright song of the conscious mind but the dark song of the unconscious, which speaks through dream and nightmare, telling us the often frightening truths that we have forgotten. The songs that come back to Maud will be

> not the songs
> of light said to wave
> through the bright hair of angels,
> but a blacker
> rasping flowering on that tongue.
>
> (7)

Kinnell is really giving himself the advice he addresses to his infant daughter: Trust the voice of the unconscious as it sings to you in the night.

In "The Hen Flower," the second of ten sections of *The Book of Nightmares,* the poet meditates on death and the human refusal to embrace death's inevitability. In the dead hen—the hen "flower"—that he holds in his hand, the poet sees a parallel to the human situation. When asked in an interview why he is so fond of bird imagery, Kinnell responded that "like everyone" he experiences "the contest between wanting to transcend and wanting to belong."[4] The hen's situation is more complicated, even, than that, and oddly comic too because, though winged and built for flight, it cannot fly. Similarly, people, though they long to transcend their own earthbound nature, are held to earth by the weight of their bodies.

At the same time that he wants to transcend the physical, the poet longs to live the purely animal life of the hen and not worry about death until it is immediately at hand.[5] "If only / we could let go," he exclaims, and "throw ourselves / on the mercy of darkness, like the hen" (11). But letting go is easy for the hen; it has no rational mind to keep it from being a good animal. In another image, though, the poet merges the two aspects of the psyche when he uses the rational mind to see the world through the body of an animal. Looking through the thin, lucent part of a ram's spealbone—the shoulder blade, a bone sometimes used by primitives as a means of divination—he has a vision of nature and natural processes unchanged by death:

> I thought suddenly
> I could read the cosmos spelling itself, . . .
>
> and in a moment,
> in the twinkling of an eye, it came to me
> the mockingbird would sing all her nights the cry of the rifle,
> the tree would hold the bones of the sniper who chose not to
>   climb down,
> the rose would bloom no one would see it,
> the chameleon longing to be changed would remain the color
>   of blood.
>
> (13)

He has his moment of existential insight, but he cannot let go, cannot accept what he sees. In despair at his vision, the poet takes the body of a chicken killed by weasels and flings it into the air in a grotesque simulation of flying, as if to assure himself that death will provide the gift of flight that the chicken—and he—was denied in life. The effect, of course, is just the opposite. Again he tells himself to "let go" and accept death, even though he is afraid of it; after all, everyone and everything is afraid of dying, of nonexistence: "even these feathers freed from their wings forever / are afraid—" (15).

Deciding to put his fear behind him, the poet, in "The Shoes of Wandering," begins his existential quest. Where is he going? He knows only that he must first lose his way. What is he looking for? He knows only that he will not find it. His quest is not his alone but the quest everyone makes in trying to come to terms with life. In what seems to be a reference to the archetypal nature of his search, the poet goes to a Salvation Army store and, after sampling "these shoes strangers have died from" (19), he buys a pair for his journey. Wearing the used shoes, walking "on the steppingstones / of someone else's wandering" (19), he trusts the instinctive wisdom of the body. When he becomes frightened that he may have lost the way, he remembers the Crone who said "the first step . . . / *shall be / to lose the way*" (19). To find what he is seeking, he will have to forsake the established paths of the rational mind and pick his way across the "swampland" (21) of the unconscious. As he walks down the road, the "wings of dust" around his feet hint at the possibility of a limited transcendence rising from the fear of death. The poet expounds on the connection between wings and feet when he goes on to ask:

> Is it the foot,
> which rubs the cobblestones
> and snakestones all its days, this lowliest
> of tongues, whose lick-tracks tell
> our history of errors to the dust behind,
> which is the last trace in us
> of wings?

(21–22)

The urge to transcend has been, in many ways, deflected into an earthbound restlessness. But the quest is both internal and external; it is not solipsistic. If it were, the poet would have a much easier time deluding himself about his ability to transcend himself. But his sense of the outside world is too sharp for any such self-deception. Also, he is clearly aware of the dangers of solipsism and is prepared to avoid them. Though he "longs for the mantle / of the great wanderers" (22) of myth and legend who always, whatever mistakes they made, found the way, he knows the Crone—the outside voice—is right when she tells him, "*you will feel all your bones / break / over the holy waters you will never drink*" (23).

The problem of delusion is examined in more detail in section 4, "Dear Stranger Extant in Memory by the Blue Juniata."

In this section, Kinnell reacts to the claims of mystics with irony and some mockery, but it is irony that is sympathetic and even partially self-directed because he would like to believe in these shortcuts to the infinite. Kinnell quotes, in the poem, from letters he has received from Virginia, a mystic. Explaining who Virginia is, Kinnell says in an interview:

> Virginia is an actual person I've had a long correspondence with. She is a mystic, a seer. She is one of those born without the protective filtering device that allows the rest of us to see this humanized, familiar world as if it were all there is. She sees past the world and lives in the cosmos.[6]

This statement may at first sound like approval of Virginia, but, though Kinnell does no doubt admire her, it is worth pointing out that their first and only meeting was unsuccessful. Through letters, Virginia and Kinnell had to "reestablish an intimacy, though we now knew it was in part illusory, being purely platonic."[7] The same criticism applies to Virginia's mysticism, which leads her to reject the world she actually lives in. While Kinnell is compelled by courtesy to be polite in his statements about the actual Virginia, the stance of the poem, as I read it, is that Virginia, with her single-minded commitment to the cosmos, is as wrong as those who can only see the world "as if it were all there is."

Two letters from Virginia are quoted in the fourth section of *The Book of Nightmares*. In the first of them she describes a session of automatic writing and her reaction to it. As her hand grows numb, she finds herself drawing, without conscious control, circles, figure eights, and mandalas. She drops the pencil, tries to relax, and then:

> I felt my mouth open. My tongue moved, my breath wasn't my own. The whisper which forced itself through my teeth said, Virginia, your eyes shine back to me from my own world. O God, I thought. My breath came short, my heart opened. O God, I thought, now I have a demon lover. (28)

The sentence about the demon lover is wonderfully comic. That is not to imply, however, that Kinnell does not sympathize very deeply with Virginia's desire to be one with the universe; indeed, he shares it. But he realizes that desire comes at the expense of the body. Virginia herself admits as much in her second letter when she says,

> God is my enemy. He gave me lust and joy and cut off my hands. My brain is smothered with his blood. I asked why should I love this body I fear. He said, It is so lordly, it can never be shaped again-dear, shining casket . . . Forgive my blindness. (30–31)

Virginia seems to be apologizing for her earlier excesses in response to Kinnell's yearning but cautious question: "Can it ever be true— / all bodies, one body, one light / made of everyone's darkness together?" (30).

As if to reemphasize that his journey is inward, section 5, "In the Hotel of Lost Light," opens with the speaker still in the bed he was sleeping in when, in section 3, he began his journey. Having taken the Crone's advice and lost the way that is illuminated by the light of the intellect, he resides now "in the Hotel of Lost Light." While lying in bed in his room, he sees and identifies himself with a fly

> whining his wings,
> concentrated wholly on
> *time, time,* losing his way worse
> down the downward-winding stairs, his wings
> whining for life as he shrivels
> in the gaze
> from the spider's clasped forebrains, the abstracted
> stare
> in which even the nightmare spatters out its horrors
> and dies.
>
> (35)

The poet lost on his inward quest is represented by the fly lost on its downward spiral, and what makes the fly shrink is the "abstracted stare"—that comes from the spider's brain. The proposed analogy is that the conscious mind is to the unconscious mind as a spider is to a fly: the latter is the prey of the former.

But Kinnell also realizes that the conscious mind is indispensable to our understanding of our situation and that the light it provides must be brought to bear, sympathetically, on the nurturing darkness of the unconscious. The rub is that light shone on darkness destroys the darkness. The poet's task—the human task—is to reconcile the irreconcilable.

"The Dead Shall Be Raised Incorruptible," section 6, is a grim consideration of what happens when the healthy impulses of the unconscious are repressed by adherence to a conscious creed. The result is "Christian man," who revels in violence and death. The biblical quotation that Kinnell takes for the title of this section pinpoints the false reasoning that has led to the Christian susceptibility to violence. Saying that "the dead shall be raised incorruptible" implies that people in their human, embodied form are corrupt—that mortality and moral failing are intrinsically linked. Kinnell maintains, in other words, that Christianity is based on contempt for the body. This section also seeks to establish a Freudian connection between anality and "Christian man," who is afflicted by, as Kinnell speaks for him, "my iron will, my fear of love, my itch for money, and my madness" (44). The madness derives from Christian man's development being arrested in the anal phase, something that is made clear in the beginning of the section, where the speaker sees a corpse smoking in a field and reacts with a list of words that make explicit the connections between death, dirt, food, and money:

> carrion,
> caput mortuum,
> orts,
> pelf,
> fenks,
> sordes,
> gurry dumped from hospital trashcans.

(41)

At the center of this emphasis on decay and scenes of warfare is a savage attack on the mentality that has produced these abominations. In a tirade derived from Villon's *Testament,* which he has translated into English, Kinnell speaks as Christian man in "the Twentieth Century of my trespass on earth" (42). He recounts the people whom he has killed, including "a whole continent of red men for living in unnatural community / and at the same time having relations with the land" (42). Later in his testament, in one of the sharpest stabs of the volume, he leaves "my flesh to the advertising man, / the anti-prostitute, who loathes human flesh for money" (43).

There is something, though, some living essence, that resists death. An unidentified voice, apparently that of a wounded GI in Vietnam, says:

> *my neck broken I ran*
> *holding my head up with both hands I ran*
> *thinking the flames*
> *the flames may burn the oboe*
> *but listen buddy boy they can't touch the notes!*

(44)

The same point is made, even more dramatically, by an image that frames this section of the book; the section begins and ends with the image of a burning corpse, perhaps a victim of napalm: "*Lieutenant! / This corpse will not stop burning!*" (41 and 45).

After the nightmare of section 6, the poet turns to his daughter, and his love for her, as Robert Langbaum points out,[8] restores him: "my broken arms heal themselves around you" (49). Section 7 primarily consists of the poet's meditations on his daughter and his advice to her. Remembering when he heard her tell a flower not to die, he says he would, if he could, keep her from dying. But, by calling her with odd and compelling tenderness "*O corpse-to-be*" (50), he acknowledges that she—like everyone—will die:

> perhaps this is the reason you cry,
> this the nightmare you wake screaming from:
> being forever
> in the pre-trembling of a house that falls.

(50)

Already she seems to grasp and be disturbed by the existential realization that life has no intrinsic meaning.

As Maud grows, the poet sees her entering the Freudian anal phase, in which the mind strives to dominate, even exclude, nature; he sees that she might become estranged from nature and the body, might even become as dangerously divorced from nature as to be like "Christian man." He remembers a time when, in a restaurant, Maud climbed into his lap and cried at the food, "*caca! caca! caca!*" (50). The child reacts so enthusiastically to the restraints of the anal phase that Kinnell fears she might, like Christian man, get stuck there, confusing nourishment and excrement. The connection is made much clearer when Kinnell describes the reaction of the other diners to his daughter's cry: "each spoonful / stopped, a moment, in midair, in its withering / steam" (50). The image evokes the opening lines of the previous section, lines that are followed by the list of archaic or unusual words that have associations with anality: "A piece of flesh gives off / smoke in the field" (41).

Kinnell can foresee a time when natural maturing processes will cut Maud off from nature. He imagines her standing in a field,

> the raindrops
> hitting you on the fontanel
> over and over, and you standing there
> unable to let them in.
>
> (51)

When and if this alienation occurs, he advises Maud to let her knowledge of death and "the sorrows / to come" cause her to embrace the present. In short, his advice is carpe diem:

> learn to reach deeper
> into the sorrows
> to come—to touch
> the almost imaginary bones
> under the face, to hear under the laughter
> the wind crying across the black stones. Kiss
> the mouth
> which tells you, *here,*
> *here is the world.* This mouth. This laughter. These temple bones.
> The still undanced cadence of vanishing.
>
> (52)

The insight implicit in this passage is stated explicitly as the section ends. Out of the pain and suffering caused by death there arises one compensation: "the wages of dying is love" (53).

From this crucial insight, the poet progresses to "The Call Across the Valley of Not-Knowing," a title that brings to mind Kierkegaard's "leap to faith." Though Kinnell does not leap across his valley, he calls across it and receives in reply intimations that harmony is possible in the world beyond. Occasionally he experiences something that lets him sense the possibility of wholeness, as he did once while in love with a woman whom he thinks of as the other half that completes his divided nature. The allusion, of course, is to Plato's speculation that the two sexes were once united beings whose union made them powerful enough to challenge the gods. Kinnell found, briefly, the half that made him whole but had to leave her because of "cowardice / loyalties, all which goes by the name of 'necessity' " (58)—reasons in which mind dominates instinct.

Expanding on the idea that "the wages of dying is love," he sees that it is death and suffering that give us the power to reach, temporarily, beyond ourselves and feel flashes of oneness, even though we are not with the exact other half we are looking for and have to settle for our "misfit":

> it must be the wound, the wound itself,
> which lets us know and love,
> which forces us to reach out to our misfit
> and by a kind
> of poetry of the soul, accomplish,
> for a moment, the wholeness the drunk Greek
> extrapolated from his high
> or flagellated out of an empty heart,
> that purest,
> most tragic concumbence, strangers
> clasped into one, a moment, of their moment on earth.

(58)

The union of two people in love and in sex is the closest people come to experiencing the integration of mind and body, but it is also tragic—it will not last, it hints at a unity that everywhere else eludes those seeking it. But in one such moment of love

Kinnell has a vision of total integration. He thinks of a time when he and his wife were young and "not yet / dipped into the acids / of the craving for anything" (58). They lay under a pear tree, "on the grass of the knowledge / of graves" (59), where they felt perfect harmony of mind and body, felt the perfect interpretation of the two opposing aspects of the self:

> And the brain kept blossoming
> all through the body, until the bones themselves could think,
> and the genitals sent out wave after wave of holy desire
> until even the dead brain cells
> surged and fell in god-like, androgynous fantasies—
> and I understand
> the unicorn's phallus could have risen, after all,
> directly out of thought itself.
>
> (59)

As if to emphasize that this vision is a vision and not the normal state of affairs, the poet recounts the story of a Southern sheriff, who, while booking the poet for participating in a civil rights march, curses and spits. What he remembers most about the sheriff, though, is "the care, the almost loving, / animal gentleness of his hand on my hand" (59) as he was fingerprinted. The sheriff's racist beliefs have overwhelmed and perverted his natural kindness, or, to put it another way, his mind has been tainted by pernicious ideas that have squelched the natural goodness that still resides in his body. He has let his mind become so alienated from his body that, in effect, he no longer has a body:

> Better than the rest of us, he knows
> the harshness of that cubicle
> in hell where they put you
> with all your desires undiminished, and with no body to
>   appease them.
>
> (59–60)

Cut off from the body, he is cut off from that which brings people together, that which affirms life even in the face of death. If we listen, even standing in a field "where the flesh /

swaddles its skeleton a last time / before the bones go their way without us," we still might hear

> even then,
> the bear call
> from his hillside—a call, like ours, needing
> to be answered—and the dam-bear
> call back across the darkness
> of the valley of not-knowing
> the only word tongues shape without intercession,
>
> *yes . . . yes . . . ?*

(61)

The only word the body forms without the intercession of the brain is one of affirmation, and that is the instinctive response of one creature to another.

If section 8 considers the relationship of humans to the beyond, "The Path Among the Stones" explores the relationship of people to the present, inanimate world, and the poet ponders the curious fact that he himself has been inanimate and will be again. At one point he speaks of arrowheads; they are

> stones
> which shuddered and leapt forth
> to give themselves into the broken hearts
> of the living,
> who gave themselves back, broken, to the stones.

(65)

Later, in an image that provides the descent into the underworld of this inner epic, the poet imagines entering the earth—a reversal of the arrowhead entering the human body. Going down into the earth, he encounters an old man who is foolishly using his intellect—the light at his forehead—in an attempt to avoid death. Inevitably he fails:

> An old man, a stone
> lamp at his forehead, squats
> by his hell-flames, stirs into
> his pot

> chopped head
> of crow, strings of white light,
> opened tail of peacock, dressed
> body of canary, robin breast
> dragged through the mud of battlefield, wrung-out
> blossom of caput mortuum flower—salts
> it all down with sand
> stolen from the upper bells of hourglasses . . .
>
> (67)

The amused irony of "salts it all down" reveals the poet's response to the old man's efforts. The attempt, by logic, to conjure from their dead bodies the birds' ability to fly, and therefore to transcend the world, is doomed to failure, as is the attempt to extract immortality from the unexpended sand in the top section of the hourglass. All these efforts, the poet says, result in "nothing. / Always nothing" (67). Immediately, however, he sees that something is gained by the striving, even, perhaps especially, if failure is unavoidable. Climbing up from the underground, he realizes the struggle has taken him to the essence of life: "I find myself alive / in the whorled / archway of the fingerprint of all things" (68).

At this insight, "the hunger / to be new lifts off" his soul (68); at long last he seems to have reconciled himself to mortality. He sees in the sacrifice of his life, a sacrifice every human has to make, the chance for a greater realization of self than would otherwise be possible:

> Somewhere
> in the legends of blood sacrifice
> the fatted calf
> takes the bonfire into his arms, and he
> burns it.
>
> (68)

To understand this enigmatic passage, I find an observation by Jungian scholar Marie Louise von Franz helpful. Speaking of sacrifice, von Franz says, "It is *the* possibility for the ego to experience the superior presence and reality of the self."[9] By suffering, the ego realizes that it is not paramount but is part of a larger whole; and by sacrifice it acknowledges that fact. There-fore, it is through suffering and sacrifice that people move toward the integration of the psyche. This pragmatic insight is what the book has been working toward throughout the first nine sections.

With "Lastness," the tenth and final section, the book comes full circle; but its movement more closely resembles a Möbius strip than it does a circle. While the setting the poet has re-turned to is more or less the same—the fire he started in the first section is "somewhere behind me" (71)—and while time has passed, what seems to be the same bear is performing what seem to be the same actions he performed then. This odd wrin-kle in time points up the inner nature of the poet's journey. He returns to the same place and events and finds that though they have remained the same, he has changed. He has a more pro-found and empathetic feeling for the world around him. His mind reaches out and he becomes the bear he is watching. The scene also suggests the ease that the poet has acquired with the natural side of himself:

> He sniffs the sweat
> in the breeze, he understands
> a creature, a death-creature
> watches from the fringe of the trees,
> finally he understands
> I am no longer there, he himself
> from the fringe of trees watches
> a black bear
> get up, eat a few flowers, trudge away, . . .
>
> (71–72)

By imagination, he breaks down the subject-object dichotomy and abridges his alienation from the world outside himself. The circular movement of the volume takes the speaker back to where he began, but in his internal odyssey he has come out in a different place. The process of suffering has allowed him the opportunity to acquire knowledge, perhaps wisdom, and to achieve glimpses of himself as a whole person.

But that sense of unity is momentary and far from absolute. About this last section, the poet asserts:

> This is the tenth poem
> and it is the last. It is right
> at the last, that one
> and zero
> walk off together,
> walk off the end of these pages together,
> one creature
> walking away side by side with the emptiness.

(73)

This stunning and witty image powerfully brings together the ideas of individuation and death, personal oneness and existential emptiness. To some extent, then, the dichotomy that has defined his struggle through the first nine sections of the book is resolved. He has achieved some integration of his own psyche, but then there rises a new dichotomy: The meaning-hungry individual lives in a world devoid of inherent meaning, but in the end the poet, accepting that emptiness with Zen-like composure attains a stronger sense of his oneness than he has had before.

How, then, does this knowledge reflect itself in an attitude toward life? How does a sense of oneness exist "side by side with the emptiness"? The answer is embodied in the image of a sky diver who is both one and divided as he plummets through the air toward the ground, as we—all of us—plummet through life toward death. His life is a

> concert of one
> divided among himself,
> this earthward gesture
> of the sky-diver, the worms
> on his back still spinning forth
> and already gnawing away
> the silks of his loves, who could have saved him,
> this free floating of one
> opening his arms into the attitude
> of flight, as he obeys necessity and falls . . .

(75)

He is compelled to assume the "attitude / of flight," (75), though he knows the transcendence he longs for is impossible.

The best he can hope for is that the worms, which represent his fear of death, don't eat away the parachute of "his loves, who could have saved him."

The image here becomes a bit ungainly as the poet tries to jam too much suggestion into it. But even this awkward exactitude points up a strength of the book: Kinnell never slides into a facile vision of mystical unity. And what tenuous unity he does attain is matched by the emptiness without. But when the one and the zero, the individual and his emptiness, join hands, they are no longer at odds, the human railing at his own death, anguishing over the lack of meaning in the world, and lamenting the failure of love. The emptiness no longer diminishes the individual; instead it enlarges him. By a form of irrational mathematics, the one added to the zero produces not one—the answer of conventional mathematics—but a figure ten times the value of the individual standing by himself.

NOTES

1. Galway Kinnell, *Walking Down the Stairs: Selections from Interviews* (Ann Arbor: University of Michigan Press, 1978), 23.

2. Galway Kinnell, *The Book of Nightmares* (Boston: Houghton Mifflin, 1971), 3. Page citations of all subsequent quotations from this book will be given parenthetically in the text of the essay.

3. Other instances of Wordsworth's influence on Kinnell are mentioned in Robert Langbaum, "Galway Kinnell's *The Book of Nightmares*," *American Poetry Review* 8 (March–April 1979): 30–31.

4. Galway Kinnell, "An Interview with Galway Kinnell," conducted by Thomas Gardner, *Contemporary Literature* 20 (1979): 427.

5. Langbaum, 30.

6. Kinnell, *Walking Down the Stairs,* 108.

7. Kinnell, *Walking Down the Stairs,* 109.

8. Langbaum, 31.

9. Marie Louise von Franz, *C. G. Jung: His Myth in our Time,* trans. William H. Kennedy (New York: Putnam, 1975), 229.

"My Only Swerving": Sentimentality, Poetry, and Animals

Before this century poets who chose to write about animals wrote mainly about birds. There are some things basically poetic about birds: They are pretty, they sing, and they can fly. And if their ability to sing makes them easily emblematic of the poet, their ability to fly makes them immediate and compact symbols of the ancient, human desire to transcend our earthbound nature. But one seldom feels of the romantic poets, say, that their birds are real birds. Instead they are points of poetic departure. Keats's nightingale serves to call him momentarily into pure "fancy," while Shelley is even more straightforward about his Neoplatonic skylark: "Bird thou never wirt." But in contemporary American poetry there are suddenly a lot of poems about animals traditionally outside the reach of human sympathy, poems about reptiles, amphibians, rodents, game animals, and predators, even insects. The shift in sensibility coincides with a shift in the perception of what the human position toward nature should be. Separated from nature by the growing urbanization of their country, most Americans now feel they should be conservators of nature rather than users of it.

In contemporary America, we have, for the most practical purposes, conquered nature, and animals whose depredations were once feared now live at our sufferance—in zoos and wildlife refuges. As Philip Levine says in the title of a poem, "animals are passing from our lives."[1] When we encounter truly wild animals in our daily lives it is a surprise, and often they are dead

From *Syracuse Scholar* 5 (Spring 1984): 5–14.

and lying beside the road, domesticated, as it were, by the machine in the garden. Almost never do we encounter a dangerous animal—a wolf, a mountain lion, a wolverine, a bear. And when we do see one we do not—unless we are hunters and rather unusual ones at that—share the impulse Thoreau had in his famous confrontation with a woodchuck near Walden Pond. The last thing that would occur to most contemporary Americans would be to fall on the woodchuck and devour it. When, in "Woodchucks," Maxine Kumin encounters the same animals as Thoreau did the result is much different. Because she fails to destroy with a "knockout bomb" the woodchucks that are ravaging her garden, she resorts to potting them with a rifle.[2] Suddenly, at the end of the poem, the speaker, feeling guilty for what she has done, laments that the woodchucks would not "die unseen / gassed underground in the quiet Nazi way." While the comparison indicates effectively the depth of the poet's guilt at what she has done to nature, at another level it reveals her failure to put the incident in its proper perspective: The implicit comparison of three dead woodchucks to twelve million dead humans is sensational and grossly out of whack. It is not a mistake Thoreau would have made, though his response was instinctual, symbolic, and one that he did not act on.

Thoreau's impulse toward participatory reverence now seems not just atavistic but inappropriate, as do similar impulses in Hemingway and Faulkner. More emblematic of our time is the existential reverence of the observer that one finds in Annie Dillard's *Pilgrim at Tinker Creek,* or at an even more extreme remove in Peter Matthiessen's *The Snow Leopard,* in which the author *fails* to see the animal he has gone to observe. The relative rarity of woodchucks, and wildlife in general, has engendered a certain hands-off reverence, but that rarity has grown directly out of man's past actions—and has resulted in a distinct ambivalence toward what has come to represent "nature" in our urban lives. At the core of the ambivalence is a mixture of guilt and romanticism that Gary Snyder points to in *Earth House Hold:* "For Americans 'nature' means wilderness, the untamed realm of total freedom—not brutish and nasty, but beautiful and terrible. Something is always eating at the human heart like acid: it is the knowledge of what we have done to our continent."[3] While the tension produced by simultaneously romanticizing nature and feeling guilty about what has been done to it has charged many poems with intensity, it has also put a strain on the poetry—a strain that frequently manifests itself as sentimentality.

When asked in an interview about his fondness for writing about small animals, Richard Eberhart answered by referring to Edmund Burke: "He has the idea that beauty is small, round and smooth. Small animals are more beautiful than big animals."[4] The distinction Burke makes is between the beautiful and the sublime, and it is instructive to consider both sides of the aesthetic problem, something Eberhart slides over. In his *Philosophical Enquiry into the Origin of Our Ideas of the Sublime and Beautiful,* Burke says:

> In the animal creation, out of our own species, it is the small we are inclined to be fond of; little birds, and some of the smaller kinds of beasts. A great beautiful thing, is a manner of expression scarcely ever used; but that of a great ugly thing, is very common. There is a wide difference between admiration and love. The sublime, which is the cause of the former, always dwells on great objects, and terrible; the latter on small ones, and pleasing; we submit to what we admire, but we love what submits to us; in one we are forced, in the other we are flattered into compliance. In short the ideas of the sublime and the beautiful stand on foundations so different, that it is hard, I had almost said impossible, to think of reconciling them in the same subject, without considerably lessening the effect of the one or the other upon the passions.[5]

Snyder's contention that Americans view nature as both "beautiful and terrible" parallels almost exactly Burke's distinction between the beautiful and the sublime. The ambivalence that Americans feel toward nature gives rise, then, to aesthetic difficulties.

Poems about the deaths of small animals, which is what I want to look at most closely, have become increasingly common in American poetry. But the poems, by the nature of their subject, attempt something Burke says is almost impossible: They attempt to bring together in one poem the beautiful—a small animal—and the sublime—death. The result quite often is poems that go awry, the speaker's reactions veering wildly out of proportion to their immediate cause. And while Snyder points out the historical and ecological background to these reactions, there are also psychological ambivalences to be considered.

A good poem in which to examine these issues is Eberhart's "The Groundhog." Walking in a field the poet sees a dead groundhog. How does he respond? His "senses shook"; "the fever arose, became a flame," and through his frame there runs "a sunless trembling."[6] Failing to control "the passion of the blood," he sinks to his knees, "Praying for joy in the sight of decay." Returning a year later, the poet finds the "bony sodden hulk" but is no longer moved by it; his mind has walled off the first, highly emotional response. When he returns a third and final time, the groundhog is gone. This time he is able to think about the death in the abstract contexts of history and philosophy. But both types of response—emotional and intellectual—are inadequate in the face of death. With one hand held across his "withered heart," he thinks

> of China and of Greece.
> Of Alexander in his tent;
> Of Montaigne in his tower,
> Of Saint Theresa in her wild lament.

The poem is emotionally out of balance. The movement from a dead groundhog to, in the last four lines, China and Greece, and Alexander, Montaigne, and Saint Theresa is breathtakingly unjustified by the internal logic of the poem up to that point. When, at the end, the poem tries to step up from the beautiful to the sublime, the object—the dead groundhog—won't bear the weight. The poem attempts to produce the desired effect by fury of language and wild extrapolation of geographical, historical, philosophical, and religious implications. The strain that results is, I think, obvious.

ɹ☙

This out-of-balance response is not limited to Eberhart. To take only fairly prominent examples, something similar happens in

Richard Wilbur's "The Death of a Toad," Alan Dugan's "Funeral Oration for a Mouse," and Theodore Roethke's "The Meadow Mouse." In each poem the death or vulnerability of the animal is extrapolated into the human realm and the emotional response grows until it is all out of proportion to what elicited it. The poems, then, are sentimental, if we accept I. A. Richards's simple and elegant definition of sentimentality: "A response is sentimental if it is too great for the occasion."[7]

Wilbur, Dugan, and Roethke—like Eberhart—attempt to put their emotional responses in perspective, though they use humor instead of pure intellectualization. But in each case the attempt collapses. Considering a toad that has lost a leg to a lawn mower, Wilbur playfully alludes to the dead toad's returning, in death, to "lost Amphibia's emperies" but quickly switches to a serious tone, too serious for the occasion.[8] Dying, the toad turns:

> Toward misted and ebullient seas
> And cooling shores, toward lost Amphibia's emperies.
> Day dwindles, drowning, and at length is gone
> In the wide and antique eyes, which still appear
> To watch, across the castrate lawn.
> The haggard daylight steer.

The death of the toad affects the world. This isn't just the pathetic fallacy—it is the pathetic fallacy operating in sympathy for a toad. J. D. Salinger defines sentimentality as "giving to a thing more tenderness than God gives it,"[9] and while God may be aware of the fall of every sparrow he does not cause the sun to become "haggard" and grass infertile as a consequence.

Theodore Roethke is more affectionate to the small animal he encounters in "The Meadow Mouse" than Wilbur is to his toad. Out walking in the meadow, the poet found a "baby mouse" that he took home and placed "in a shoe box stuffed in an old nylon stocking."[10] He feeds the mouse "three kinds of cheese" and gives him water in a "bottle-cap watering trough." When, after it has eaten, he approaches it, he imagines the mouse "no longer trembles / When I come close to him." Despite his hope that the mouse has come to accept his presence, when he goes out on the porch in the morning and checks the box he finds the mouse has escaped:

> Where has he gone, my meadow mouse,
> My thumb of a child that nuzzled in my palm?
> To run under the hawk's wing,
> Under the eye of the great owl watching from the elm-tree,
> To live by courtesy of the shrike, the snake, the tom-cat.

If the poem ended here, it would be a solid and balanced, if small, poem about the mouse's leaving the protection afforded by the poet and returning to its natural position in the food chain. The poem points up the changing relationship of poets to nature; it is difficult to imagine Emerson, Whitman, Hart Crane, or Eliot, as adults, keeping a mouse in a box on the back porch. But the poet's realization that the mouse has chosen to return to a situation in which it is subject to predators has a crisp sense of perspective to it. He realizes that he is foolhardy to think that the wildness can be domesticated out of nature, and he realizes that though he sees himself as a protector the mouse does not share that perception. In spite of his longing to join with it, man remains separate from nature.

But the poem does not stop here. It goes on for four more lines that greatly raise the emotional and intellectual ante:

> I think of the nestling fallen into the deep grass,
> The turtle gasping in the dusty rubble of the highway,
> The paralytic stunned in the tub, and the water rising—
> All things innocent, hapless, forsaken.

The abrupt and clumsy transition "I think" is followed by two examples from nature that limit rather than expand the story about the mouse. They serve primarily to set up the third example, the one that violently yanks the poem into the human realm. The nestling is larger than the mouse and is isolated from its natural element—the air; and the turtle, larger yet, gasps in the dust, separated from its element—water. But the leap from the turtle to the paralyzed human is too great, and it raises questions. How, for instance, does the paralytic get in this predicament? The context of the mouse's situation is provided by the poem, and it is easy enough to imagine a bird falling from its nest or a turtle wandering too far in search of water; but a paralytic who is "forsaken" in a tub of rising water can have got there only through the actions of another person. Also, though the word "innocent" raises philosophical and theological considerations that the poet may not be concerned with, it is safe to say that a human being cannot be considered innocent in the same way an animal can. And to call a paralytic in imminent danger of drowning "hapless" is simply peculiar. Surely he is more than just unlucky. But the last four lines of the poem introduce other problems as well.

The ending extends the scope of the poem way past what it has been. There is a huge qualitative difference between a mouse living under the threat of a tomcat and a paralyzed human being who is unable to escape from rising water. Everything up to the last four lines has served to emphasize the smallness and cuteness of the mouse—its beauty, to use Burke's term—and the sudden appearance of the endangered paralytic introduces the terrible, the overwhelming—the sublime. The disjunction between the beautiful and the sublime leads us, once more, to the processes of the poet's mind, and though I may be pushing the evidence further than it wants to go, the paralytic seems to me emblematic of the poet's own paralysis of will in the face of approaching and inexorable death. The first part of the poem represents his attempt to domesticate that fear by projecting it onto the body of the mouse, the "little quaker" that he has removed from the menace of "the shrike, the snake, the tom-cat." But the mouse resists the projection when it instinctively returns to the world in which it is subject to sudden and violent death. In the end, the poet's fear erupts, frighteningly, into the human realm, though it is still displaced—this time onto the body of a paralytic. The discrepancy between the meadow mouse and the emotional weight the mouse is being made to bear makes the poem sentimental, and the sentimentality arises from the poet's displacement of his own fear onto an inappropriate situation instead of confronting it head on.

Wit helps keep Alan Dugan's "Funeral Oration for a Mouse" in balance, and only when the wit is relinquished does the poem run into trouble. Like Roethke's "little quaker," Dugan's mouse is a "living diagram of fear."[11] But Dugan is fully aware that the mouse, which has been killed in a trap that he and his wife have set out, is a pest: "full of health himself / he brought diseases like a gift / to give his hosts." And when Dugan feels guilty for killing the mouse, he realizes both that the guilt is real and that it is a "minor guilt." His tone indicates that he does not blow the guilt out of its proper proportion, while, at the same time, he acknowledges the brutality of the mouse's demise:

> Lord, accept our felt though minor guilt
> for an ignoble foe and ancient sin:
> the murder of a guest
> who shared our board: just once he ate
> too slowly, dying in our trap
> from necessary hunger and a broken back.

But in dying the mouse has, in a sense, acquired knowledge denied any living creature. Even this somewhat ponderous insight is quickly undercut by the poet, who acknowledges the disparity between him and his wife and the mouse; they "pinch" and he, as a consequence, "spasms":

> Why,
> then, at that snapping sound, did we, victorious,
> begin to laugh without delight?

The poet admits his ambivalence. Though he laughs at killing the pest, it is a laugh without delight because he knows that when he goes to remove the dead mouse from the trap he will encounter not just the limp body of the mouse but also death itself. In dying the mouse assumed an aspect of the terrible that removes it from the reach of the poet's wit that has tried to diminish the terror. The mouse has become a memento mori, and the poet and his wife instinctively shy away from the idea of death; their stomachs "demanded a retreat / from our machine and its effect of death":

as if the mouse's fingers, skinnier
than hairpins and as breakable as cheese,
could grasp our grasping lives, and in
their drowning movement pull us under too,
into the common death beyond the mousetrap.

The logic of the poem, certainly, is all of a piece. The poet is fully aware that the emotion he feels is not really for the mouse; it arises because the mouse's death makes him consider his own. But the last three lines lack the wit and discerning ambivalence that charge the rest of the poem. They are, in fact, slightly leaden. The irony and wit that have kept the poem balanced between the beautiful and the sublime are dropped when the mouse's death begins to have human implications. Though the imbalance is slight, the problem is caused by the poet's inability to be as witty about his own death as he is about the mouse's. And, in the end, Dugan's wit, like Eberhart's passion, Wilbur's irony, and Roethke's strained earnestness, seems a bit like whistling in the existential dark.

❧

Just as humor and irony are used to tease away sentimentality, so too are animals that are not usually the objects of human concern—rodents and amphibians. If the poems were about kitty cats and sad-eyed puppies, the sentimentality would be glaringly clear, and the evocation of a stock response—to use another of I. A. Richards's concepts—would be too obvious. But if these poems of Eberhart, Wilbur, Roethke, and Dugan have problems, they are conceptual problems of a very high level. And if the poems are sentimental, it is in a certain sense a technical sentimentality—not the syrupy excess of emotion normally associated with the term. Just to make clear the degrees of sentimentality, it is useful to consider Rod McKuen's "Thoughts on Capital Punishment," which advocates the death penalty for running over animals:

There ought to be capital punishment for cars
that run over rabbits and drive into dogs
that commit the unspeakable, unpardonable crime
of killing a kitty-cat still in his prime.[12]

As if the image of cars being executed isn't enough, McKuen goes on to evoke the pathos of Mrs. Badger waiting for a husband who will never return because "he didn't know what automobiles are about." In case we begin to wonder if this is a parody of sentimental poetry, the poet ends the poem by looking us right in the eye and informing us, "Who kills a man kills a bit of himself / But a cat too is an extension of God." McKuen is, of course, a convenient, and deserving, whipping boy, but his poem does, by contrast, point up the virtues of the other poems whose sentimentality occurs at a much higher level.

The sentimental reaction to dead animals is, as you might expect, hard to find in poets with rural backgrounds. It is more or less absent from the work of Robert Frost, Gary Snyder, Wendell Berry, and Southern poets in general. But as America becomes ever more urban and suburban, I suspect there will be more and more poems about the deaths of small animals, and my casual reading of literary journals backs up this intuition. The poems are a minor, literary consequence of changing relationship to nature. We no longer fear and hate mice. One mouse in the house no longer raises the specter of hundreds munching their way through the corncrib and thus threatening our very survival. The word *vermin* is almost never used anymore in its literal sense of "objectionable animals" and exists now for its metaphorical connotations. Roethke in "The Meadow Mouse" and James Wright in his "A Mouse Taking a Nap" feel as if they menace the mouse, and each feels, in varying degrees, as if he is its protector. Though Wright, for instance, admits he does not like the mouse, he takes evident pleasure in its enjoying a respite from its predators, which "are gone for a little while, hunting someone else for a little while."[13] Because we live divorced from nature and the natural cycle, when we see the harm we inflict on nature it is most often in the form of a dead small animal. The nineteenth-century literary myth that Leo Marx traces in *The Machine in the Garden* has moved into high gear in the twentieth century as advanced technology has raced across the Eden of North America. The machine has penetrated into even the most casual and domestic levels of our lives. Dugan takes no pleasure in the "machine" that killed the mouse over which he delivers his funeral oration, and William Stafford in "Traveling through the Dark"—a poem to which I will return—is aware that the car that carries him through the darkness can also destroy the animals that live there, as someone else's car already has. So thoroughly is nature subject to technology that a toad hit by a lawn mower becomes a metaphor for the current state of man's relationship with nature.

❧

But guilt at the subjugation of nature, though real and hovering in the background of many poems, does not entirely account for the deep-seated emotion that throws the poems out of whack. Machines, after all, aren't present in Eberhart's "The Groundhog" or Roethke's "The Meadow Mouse." Also, guilt about the misuse of the environment is too intellectualized to provoke such a clearly displaced response: People who resent what humanity has done to nature generally know how they feel and have no qualms about expressing those feelings. Richards, following Freud, sees sentimentality as a consequence of inhibition: "As a rule the source of such inhibitions is some painfulness attaching to the aspect of life that we refuse to contemplate."[14] The repressed emotion will, however, find a way out. And the pain the poems are hiding—I suspect, I cannot know—is the poet's fear of his own death. He displaces his fear of death onto the dead animal, and that is why the poems suddenly become anguished and why the death of the animal is treated as though it were as important as the death of a person. The smallness allows the poet to minimize death so he can try to master it. But the attempt to tuck something as overwhelming as death into a small and manageable box is bound to rupture the box. The poets in these poems are in a situation analogous to that of the young girl in Hopkins's "Spring and Fall." Facing the issue head on, Hopkins tells the girl who is grieving at the falling leaves, "It is the blight man was born for, / It is Margaret you mourn for."[15]

The psychological problem leads, in turn, to an aesthetic one. The attempt to make death manageable is an attempt to convert the sublime into the beautiful. And the attempt, by its very nature, is bound to fail because death is not subject to human domestication. Though he is not talking specifically of death, Burke warns the artist of the aesthetic problems it can pose. While admitting that the beautiful and the sublime are rarely to be found in their pure forms, he cautions against confusing the two:

> They are indeed ideas of a very different nature, one being founded on pain, the other on pleasure; and however they may vary afterwards from the direct nature of their causes, yet these causes keep up an eternal distinction between them, a distinction never to be forgotten by any whose business it is to affect the passions.[16]

Yet the distinction often is forgotten because of the natural impulse to convert, by psychological and aesthetic alchemy, the painful into the pleasurable—the impulse to deny death.

を

Is it possible, then, to write a totally successful nonironic poem about the death of a small animal? Burke would be dubious, and I cannot think of an example that would convince him it can be done. Even William Stafford in "Traveling through the Dark" has to write about a fairly large animal to make his poem work.

"Traveling through the Dark" is one of the few successful poems dealing with the deaths of animals, and it owes much of its success to Stafford's exquisite awareness of the significance of the dead deer he finds beside the road. He does not attempt to diminish the importance of the animal's death, but neither does he attempt to make more of it than it is. When he finds the dead deer, the poet is tempted to sentimentalize it—to "swerve"—but he knows that to do so would be to endanger those who will come behind him.[17] Precisely because the deer's dead body is dangerous, the poet must make a hard choice about what to do, and the danger the deer poses is a result of its size. In other words, Stafford gives himself a technical, aesthetic advantage that other poets deny themselves: He writes about a larger animal than they do. The deer is very close to human size and is, therefore, suspended between the sublime and the beautiful. If anything, it is closer to the sublime. And the sublimity of the animal is accentuated by the fact that it is dangerous to those who might hit it and lose control of their cars. Because of its size, it has to be treated with some measure of thought and dignity. It is substantial. It has to be *pushed* into the river; it cannot simply be kicked off into the underbrush, as you might do to a dead rabbit if you worried about it at all:

> I stood in the glare of the warm exhaust turning red;
> around our group I could hear the wilderness listen.
>
> I thought hard for us all—my only swerving—,
> then pushed her over the edge into the river.

Though he is, in fact, tempted to swerve—to make more of it than he should—the speaker's emotions are totally appropriate to the occasion. To those that follow, he has an existential obligation, as it were, to remove the deer, even though he did not cause it to be there. He treats the deer with respect, he is attentive enough to notice she is "large in the belly" and then to touch her belly and find out she is pregnant. Even the doe's pregnancy and the fact that the unborn fawn is still alive, which in a lesser poet might strengthen the impulse to sentimentality, serve as a temptation that he resists.

This is not to say he is unmoved by the situation. As the poet realizes the implications of the doe's warm belly, the poem intensifies, but the intensity parallels the poet's own deepening understanding: "her fawn lay there waiting, / alive, still, never to be born." He hesitates. But his first commitment is to the people who might be injured if he lets his emotions prevail to no purpose. The poem strikes an astoundingly sure balance between sorrow and responsibility, between the instinctive emotional response and the need to do what must be done. And the balance is all the more impressive in that it does not become self-justifying or sanctimonious. If the poet doesn't become overemotional, neither does he minimize the deer's death. He hesitates, thinks seriously about the situation, and realizes there is nothing he can do. Then, putting the incident in the larger perspective, he puts aside his own feelings and reacts for the good of others: "I thought hard for us all—my only swerving—, / then pushed her over the edge into the river." There is deep emotion in the poem but not a trace of sentimentality; every emotion grows out of the situation and is perfectly in proportion to what the situation calls for. The poem is so clear-eyed about the world and emotionally responsible about what it sees that it can properly be called wise, and that, for all their considerable virtues, is not true of the other poems.

NOTES

1. Philip Levine, *Not This Pig* (Middletown, CT: Wesleyan University Press, 1968), 79.

2. Maxine Kumin, *Our Ground Time Here Will Be Brief* (New York: Penguin Books, 1982), 155.

3. Gary Snyder, *Earth House Hold: Technical Notes and Queries to Fellow Dharma Revolutionaries* (New York: New Directions, 1969), 119.

4. Richard Eberhart, *Of Poetry and Poets* (Urbana: University of Illinois Press, 1979), 28.

5. Edmund Burke, *A Philosophical Enquiry into the Origin of Our Ideas of the Sublime and Beautiful*, ed. J. T. Boulton (London: Routledge and Kegan Paul, 1958), 113–14.

6. Richard Eberhart, *Collected Poems, 1930–1976* (New York: Oxford University Press, 1977), 23.

7. I. A. Richards, *Practical Criticism: A Study of Literary Judgment* (New York: Harcourt Brace, 1929), 244.

8. Richard Wilbur, *New and Collected Poems* (New York: Harcourt Brace Jovanovich, 1988), 320.

9. J. D. Salinger, as quoted in Daniel Halpern, "The Pursuit of Suffering," *Antaeus* 40/41 (Winter–Spring 1981): 432.

10. Theodore Roethke, *The Collected Poems of Theodore Roethke* (New York: Anchor Books, 1975), 219.

11. Alan Dugan, *Collected Poems* (New Haven: Yale University Press, 1969), 39.

12. Rod McKuen, "Thoughts on Capital Punishment," in X. J. Kennedy, *An Introduction to Poetry*, 3d ed. (Boston: Little, Brown, 1974), 249–50.

13. James Wright, *This Journey* (New York: Vintage Books, 1982), 71.

14. Richards, *Practical Criticism*, 253.

15. Gerard Manley Hopkins, "Spring and Fall," *The Poems of Gerard Manley Hopkins*, 4th ed. Edited by W. H. Gardner and N. H. MacKenzie (New York: Oxford University Press, 1967), 89.

16. Burke, *A Philosophical Enquiry*, 124.

17. William Stafford, *Traveling Through the Dark* (New York: Harper and Row, 1962), 11.

"The Honest Work of the Body": Jorie Graham's *Erosion*

The problem of the separateness of the mind and body has been a philosophical commonplace since at least the times of the pre-Socratic philosophers, but its antiquity does nothing to diminish its everyday significance in our lives, nor its importance as a continuing theme in poetry. After all, the problem of the flawed nature of incarnation, as the immaculate idea becomes corrupted by taking form, is one the poet confronts every day: the poem in the mind is always better than the poem that appears on the page, deformed by becoming actual. In *Erosion* Jorie Graham is deeply engaged with her perceived separateness of the mind and body, and imagery of gaps and stitching recurs obsessively as she tries to knit the two together. The book depicts the poet's attempts to shift her love of the mind, whose limitations she is well aware of, at least partially to the body. The integrated vision of the book grows, in fact, out of the poet's attempt to balance the opposed components of her psyche. Whether or not she succeeds, that struggle makes *Erosion* more than a collection of poems on a common theme; it is an evolving and coherent poetic sequence that traces the psychological dimensions of a philosophical problem.

In some ways the book unfolds like an argument—as orderly and, at times, almost as dispassionate—as the poet confesses her love for the cleanness of abstraction over the disorderliness of

---

From *Shenandoah* 46 (Summer 1996): 48–59. Excerpts from *Erosion*.

the body. But she knows that she must learn to love the body. Unlike abstraction, whose lack of physical substance is its glory, the body is alive—capable of joy and passion—and though it is subject to death it is also able to reproduce itself. In the first poem of *Erosion*, "San Sepolcro," Graham exclaims, "How clean / the mind is,"[1] and the cleanness obviously attracts her. But she quickly adds "holy grave" to her exclamation because she knows the mind is too pure to live outside its own abstractions. Its cleanness is sterile. Though the body may be subject to death, the mind, because it cannot by itself affect the world, is impotent, lifeless, and, in a sense, already dead. The poem, inviting us into the book, is also the poet's instruction to herself to leave the sterility of the mind and enter the world: "Come, we can go in. . . . / This is / what the living do: go in" (3). And it is an invitation into both the erosion of her allegiance to the mind and the erosion of the body itself. The poet knows she must acknowledge the claims of the body, but she is distrustful of it, begrudging, unwilling to accept her own dying. There is a stubborn integrity to the book as the poet resists the wisdom of her insight. In its struggle, the book begins where most end. Instead of ending with a flash of insight, the book begins with the poet's knowledge of what she must do and then traces her attempts to accept that knowledge and live with it.

In "Scirocco," Graham visits the room in which Keats died and meditates on the grapes in the arbor outside the window. The poem deliberately evokes Keats's "Ode to Melancholy" by stressing the mutability of the physical and also by adopting and then transforming Keats's image of sensory pleasure being fulfilled in melancholy by him "whose strenuous tongue / Can burst Joy's grape against his palate fine." The grape must, of course, be broken before it can be enjoyed, but once it is broken the joy is almost at an end. Graham sees in the grapes the sheer vulnerability of flesh, its impermanence. Outside the window, "you can hear the scirocco / working / the invisible," and in the arbor:

> the stark hellenic
> forms
> of grapes have appeared.

```
        They'll soften
    till weak enough
        to enter

    our world, translating
        helplessly
    from the beautiful
        to the true.
```

(8–9)

Ringing a change on the famous final couplet of "Ode on a Grecian Urn" in which Keats insists "Beauty is truth, truth beauty," Graham laments the weakening and softening that occur as the beautiful moves "helplessly" into flawed and limited actuality. In some ways, she is a better Platonist than Keats. Her distinctions between the dualities of visible and invisible, flesh and spirit, body and mind, truth and beauty are specific variations on Plato's distinction between the concrete real and the ideal. But where Keats attempts to unify the Platonic dualism, Graham insists on the separateness of the opposed concepts. She resists the move from the perfection possible in the mind, resists softening into the imperfect limitations of the dirty fact, the thing itself:

```
            this
        is what I
    must ask you
        to imagine: wind;
    the moment
        when the wind

    drops; and grapes
        which are nothing,
    which break
        in your hands
```

(11)

Though the writing in the poem is a little fussy—notice how the semicolons in the series impede the straightforward lyricism of the lines—Graham's voice is most moving, deeply felt, and convincing in poems like this one, poems in which she laments the frailty of the flesh. But she knows that both sides of the person must be reckoned with; the flesh must be given its due and the harsh demands of the spirit must be tempered. "In What Manner the Body is United With the Soule" addresses the issue explicitly and acknowledges that the self is made up of both flesh and spirit. The self, she says:

> is an act of
>   rescue
> where the flesh has risen,
>   the spirit
> loosened. . . .

(14)

And if her heart isn't quite at one with the statement, perhaps it is because emotions often linger behind where the mind knows the heart should be.

Though the constant talk of spirit and flesh has religious overtones, they are not of a Christian nature, but rather of a puritanism thrown into hard reverse, as the poet tries to loosen the spirit. One way Graham attempts to do that is by her meditation on a sort of reverse excoriation of the flesh. In contrast to the flagellation of monks, which was supposed to subdue the flesh and free the spirit, Graham celebrates the pain of the flesh as a sensual experience—it reminds the mind that the body is still there, that it cannot be forgotten or brushed aside. In "The Age of Reason" she sees in her orchard a bird that is "anting." Over an anthill, the bird has "opened his wings" and is taking the ants up into his feathers:

> At times they'll take on
>   almost anything
> that burns, spreading
>   their wings
>
> over coals, over cigarette
>   butts,
> even, mistakenly, on bits
>   of broken glass.
> Meanwhile the light keeps
>   stroking them
>
> As if it were love.

(16)

But so deep does Graham's ambivalence toward the body run that she takes a real and strange pleasure in the pain. "Who wouldn't want," she asks,

> to take
> into the self
> something that burns
>
> or cuts, or wanders
> lost
> over the body?

(17)

Despite the author's attraction (philosophical though it may be) to the pain, the question is chilling. Most people would not want to take into their selves something that "burns // or cuts, or wanders / lost / over the body."

Elsewhere in *Erosion* birds (and other flying things) symbolize, as they often do in poetry, the human desire to transcend the limitations of the world and the body. Keats's "Ode to a Nightingale," for instance, comes easily to mind, though Keats does not—as Graham tries to—shy away from the knowledge that the desire to leave the body is a displaced longing for death. But, because she is trying to shift her allegiance from the mind to the body, she comes up with a very interesting symbol to balance the birds. Unlike birds, which leave the earth in flight, fish are ineluctably immersed in the substance of this world. In one of her finest poems, "My Garden, My Daylight," Graham meditates on the "bottom fish" her neighbor offers her and how, though they live in mud, they also acquire a kind of purity. Feeding, they drive "their bodies through the mud, / mud through their flesh. / See how white they become" (30). The bottom fish aren't as beautiful, or as good to eat, as the fish that swim up near the surface, shining in "quick schools" that are "forever trying to slur over, become water." Instead they

> belong to us
> who cannot fall out of this world
> but only deeper

into it, driving it into the white
of our eyes.

(30)

The poet, realizing she cannot hope to transcend the physical, considers immersing herself in it. What is the consequence of driving the world "into the white / of our eyes"? It is "Muddy / daylight, we utter it, we drown in it." It is an ambivalent affirmation, if an affirmation at all. The iced-down fish her neighbor offers her may not be beautiful but they are *true,* she says. The neighbor holds the fish out for her to take:

Its icy fruit
seems true,

it glows. *For free* he says
so that I can't refuse.

(31)

Musically, the poem is stunning. Through the last two stanzas Graham establishes a strongly iambic free verse to reinforce the sense of closure in the poem's movement, and the subtle interplay of *u* sounds around different consonants is masterly. But the poem—significantly—stops short of the poet's actually accepting the fish that are held out to her by her neighbor.

"My Garden, My Daylight" is, I think, a crucial poem in the book because its central image becomes an emblem for the whole book: someone is holding out a gift of flesh and the poet stands there thinking about it until the man, perhaps a bit embarrassed or confused, feels obligated to assure her it is free. Philosophically, as well as actually, he is offering her flesh, and while she says she cannot refuse, neither can she bring herself to reach out and take it. And she only gets to the point of saying she can't refuse it by concentrating on its whiteness—how it converts the mud it lives in into a type of purity. In this poem, as in the rest of the book, the speaker is extraordinarily passive, much more acted on than acting, as she responds to every stimulus by *thinking* about it, even when the proper response would simply be to say "Thank you" and accept the gift. I get a sense of a speaker radically unreconciled to the world around her, and that is manifest both in what the poem says and in the social awkwardness of the situation it describes.

To be sure, all Keats does in the great odes is think, but he achieves true negative capability; he is passionately involved with what he sees and thinks about, while Graham's eye is too wary, too suspicious of what the world has to offer. She resists this offer and can only accept it by converting it into something as clean as the mind. The danger, of course, is solipsism, and it is a danger Graham does not always avoid.

"I Watched a Snake" goes one step further than "My Garden, My Daylight" in the poet's attempt to love the body more, but it remains highly ambivalent. "Desire," she comes to realize, "is the honest work of the body," which is a slightly peculiar way to say it—a puritan's effort to love the body by proclaiming that what it does is work, and "honest work" at that. She goes on to say that passion is what rescues the sterility of the mind and ties us, as suffering humans, to the larger cycles of life:

> Passion is work
> that retrieves us,
> lost stitches. It makes a pattern of us,
> it fastens us
> to sturdier stuff
> no doubt.

(31)

But if the quick ironic fillip of that last line signals that she is dubious about the validity of her own insight, it also saves the poem from a certain preachiness it would otherwise have.

By the time she gets to the title poem, however, the poet is able to embrace with fewer reservations the idea of emptying the mind in a way that sounds vaguely Zen-inspired. "Erosion" begins:

> I would not want, I think, a higher intelligence, one
> simultaneous, cut clean
> of sequence. No,
> it is our slowness I love, growing slower,
> tapping the paintbrush against the visible,
> tapping the mind.

(56)

At the end of the poem the idea of "tapping the mind" is brought up again. Graham says she has lined up wine glasses on the windowsill and put varying amounts of water in them so she can "tap them / for music." The weather is growing colder, and she observes that the less water—the less mind—there is in the glass, "the truer / the sound." The poem ends:

> Outside the window it's starting to snow.
> It's starting to get colder.
> The less full the glass, the truer
> the sound.
> This is my song
> for the North
> coming toward us.
>
> (57)

Though the last three lines are perhaps a bit facile, the poet edges still closer to her goal of letting go of her allegiance to the mind. By emptying her mind of what she wants the world to be, she is able to play a "truer" song for the oncoming winter, which of course suggests death. Still, she resists the change. The affirmation is a negative one. She celebrates the emptying of the mind, but not yet does she celebrate the filling of the body.

The idea of only the body's being able, in the face of death, to provide any comfort, no matter how inadequate, is approached in the book's penultimate poem, "At Luca Signorelli's Resurrection of the Body," a poem of great accomplishment. As she examines the painting, the poet concentrates on the eagerness with which the spirits seek to become embodied:

> See how they hurry
>   to enter
> their bodies,
>   these spirits.
> Is it better, flesh,
>   that they
> should hurry so?
>
> (74)

But notice how skeptical the poet remains as she answers her own question with another question:

                The artist
has tried to make it so each tendon
        they press
to re-enter
        is perfect. But is it
perfection
        they're after,
pulling themselves up
        through the soil

into the weightedness, the color,
        into the eye
of the painter?

(74–75)

Of course perfection is not what they are after. As spirits free of the flawed and encumbering body, they have perfection, but they willingly renounce perfection for the chance to be made incarnate. Why do they want so ardently to be flesh? Graham doesn't say. She isn't sure. But she knows that if their desire is as strong as it appears, they must have compelling reasons.

Toward the end, the poem turns from the painting to Signorelli himself. Signorelli's interest in spirit becoming flesh was more than just a subject for his paintings, it was a consuming passion that led him to dissect bodies to search for the soul, looking for the true beyond the beautiful:

                But the wall
of the flesh
        opens endlessly,
its vanishing point so deep
        and receding

we have yet to find it,
        to have it
stop us. So he cut
        deeper
graduating slowly
        from the symbolic
to the beautiful. How far
        is true?

(76)

When his only son died, Signorelli also dissected him:

> It took him days
> > that deep
> caress, cutting,
> > unfastening,
>
> until his mind
> > could climb into
> the open flesh and
> > mend itself.

(77)

Exactly how Signorelli's mind, climbing into the flesh of his dead son, heals itself is left vague. In fact, something seems awry because to be healed Signorelli's mind would, it seems to me, have to climb down into the healing properties of his own flesh, opened by grief, and not into the already dead body of his son. Still, the poem implies that the integration of mind and body can begin when the mind acknowledges that the body has the power to heal, that it doesn't just erode. Even here, however, the poet maintains her stubborn integrity. She does not, to make a neat poetic statement, throw caution aside and falsely claim that she wholeheartedly embraces the body—its joys and inevitable disintegration. In the book's final poem, "The Sense of an Ending," the poet goes as far as she can at the moment. She admits that "human / souls are in a frenzy / to be born, to be brought over here through flesh" (82–83) and that somehow, ineffably, it is better to be in the body despite the ineluctable corruption of the flesh. At times, she says, she can feel the souls:

> pressing into my human frame, knocking,
>
> pushing, as if an entrance here, no matter
> > how short or broken—no matter
>
> the hundred kinds of burn, the thousand kinds
> > of rot—no matter
>
> the terrible insufficiencies of matter in the face
> > of any kind of spent
>
> time, were better than any
> > freedom, any wholeness—horribly better—even for a

single hour, no matter what,
    even for minutes, better, this heaviness, this stilled

quickness, this skin, this line
    all the way round and scaled into the jagged island

form.

(83)

Though one occasionally gets the feeling Graham's poems are executed, not written, that reservation does not apply to "The Sense of an Ending." The passionate voice in this poem—and it is the most passionate in the book—is utterly convincing.

The poems like "San Sepolcro," in which Graham writes about the joys of the mind, can be delicately intricate and rich with celebration; and those, like "The Sense of an Ending," in which she regrets the necessity of the spirit's being incarnate, speak with real and resonate anguish. But in other poems, when she makes herself try to move from her love of the mind to an appreciation of the body—as in "Erosion"—the stance seems willed, as if the poet is forcing herself to say something she doesn't believe, in the hope that if she says it with enough conviction she will come to believe it. That is to say, sometimes she says what she feels she ought to say rather than what she believes. The result is a strange stiffness running through some of the poems—the stiffness of a puritan renouncing, as an intellectual decision, a faith she still holds in her heart. And it is a harrowing irony of the book that the most passion comes through in the poems celebrating the mind, while the poems that aim to celebrate passion are stiff with intellectualizing. But from the tension that paradox produces, the book draws considerable power. The paradox may knock some individual poems awry as what is said is at variance with how it is said, but this problem does not undercut the book as a coherent poetic statement of a quest in process; if anything, it validates the author's attempt to shift her allegiance from mind to body by showing that she has correctly perceived what she needs to do. And the difficulty she has with the project underscores the integrity and courage she brings to it. The partial success of her personal quest is responsible for the greater artistic success

of her poetic quest, which embodies the disharmonious har-
mony of reality.

NOTE

1. Jorie Graham, *Erosion* (Princeton, NJ: Princeton University
Press, 1983), 2. All subsequent citations of this book will be given
parenthetically in the body of the essay.

The Glass Anvil: "The Lies of an Autobiographer"

Memory is a strange Bell—
Jubilee, and Knell.

—Emily Dickinson

Vows are dangerous. As a freshman in high school, when I read poems only for class assignments and even then reluctantly, I vowed that if I ever wrote anything as silly as a poem at least I'd never write about anything as silly as flowers. Flowers struck me as effeminate, nonutilitarian, decorative at best, and, at worst, an utter waste of time and money. As a subject for poetry they combined those shortcomings with a complete lack of serious engagement with the world and its ills. In time, I became a gardener, and as a poet I've returned again and again to the traditional subject that I so scorned, finding it fecund with meaning and rich with emotional significance. And I've enjoyed the uneasy honor of having one of my lines quoted in the Smith and Hawken gardening catalog next to a photograph of, and a paean to, a Scottish manure fork.

In college, in mild revolt against my Southern Baptist upbringing, I vowed I'd never write about religious subjects, which seemed to me artistically spent and intellectually vacant. Later, because they were all the mode in the 1960s and '70s, I vowed I wouldn't write poems about paintings. The idea of making art about art appeared to me both to be parasitic and to place the

Reprinted from *The American Scholar* 65 (Autumn 1996): 541–53. Excerpts from *The Glass Hammer.* Copyright © 1994 by Andrew Hudgins. Reprinted by permission of Houghton Mifflin Co. All rights reserved.

second work of art, the poem in this case, at an extra and enfeebling remove from life. I ended up writing a book of poems, *The Never-Ending*, that has as one of its recurring subjects the life of Christ as portrayed in paintings.

In similar fashion I vowed, because I was tired of so-called confessional poetry with its often lurid self-revelations, not to write about myself. So, probably as a result of that vow, I wrote a childhood memoir. In poems. *The Glass Hammer: A Southern Childhood*. But when I broke my vow, finally admitting that what I'd begun *was* an autobiography, I made another vow: that I, as I alone could do, would tell the honest truth. This vow was a reiteration of a vow I'd made as a child. By age twelve I'd read dozens of childhood memoirs with sentimental portraits of a loving if harried Mama, a loving if occasionally frustrated and angry Papa, and a supportive if moralistic community. Despite some obstacles, success came so easily for the gifted child that it seemed inevitable—and all I could think was that those charmed lives, fascinating as they were, were nothing like mine.

A few years later, having read dozens more childhood memoirs, I began to say, "They're lying. All those writers are just lying. Life isn't that simple." But as I thought about it I began to see that they weren't lying consciously; they just didn't remember. And I vowed then, with all the plentiful rage and gravity that a fifteen-year-old Southern boy steeped in codes of honor and manhood can bring to a vow, that if I ever wrote about my life I'd do it while I was still angry and that my book would be brutal, ruthless, scorchingly honest. I'd blow the lid off the pot, dammit.

But as soon as I began writing in earnest I realized that some lies—though now we literary sorts call them "fictions"—are inevitable. Others are merely convenient. Autobiography is in some ways a translation of actuality onto the page and in other ways it's a selective and imaginative re-creation of it, a work of art—and the two roles can go to bed together and enjoy their uneasy congress only by lying to one another. But the lies are loving lies, told with hope and good intentions, and I'd like to talk about some of the ways autobiography—or at least mine—lies. I've arranged these fictions in ascending order of transgression from misdemeanor to felony.

1. The first lie, the whitest lie, the lie that hardly troubles my conscience at all, is the lie of narrative cogency. It consists of clearing out the narrative underbrush so the story, like a flowering crab apple in a lot overgrown with sumac, can be more easily seen and appreciated. Exposition, explanation, and qualification are boring. They try the reader's patience. And with its emphasis on condensed intensity, poetry is even less tolerant of them than prose. In *The Glass Hammer* I didn't bother to explain my family's frequent moves from one Air Force base to another as my father was transferred around the country. He retired in Montgomery, Alabama, where I went to high school and college, and since I long ago decided that Montgomery was my hometown I simply set the whole book there.

And I combined characters and incidents. Here's part of a poem called "Original Sin":

> I'd watched
> hens jab the dirty silk
> of spider webs, jerk back,
> pause, flip their heads, and swallow
> live spiders. *Only a thing*
> *that's poisonous itself*
> *eats spiders,* Grandmomma said.
> And I believed her. I'd seen them
> rake each other's raw
> red flaws until they'd crippled
> or killed a bird that could
> have been themselves. Or me.
> But when Grandmomma marched
> out to the tree, I followed
> and crowed at the hens as she
> grabbed one bird by the neck
> and snapped her wrist. Waist-high,
> held out away from her,
> the dead bird walked on air
> and flapped. I ran behind,
> crowed, clucked, and flapped my arms
> triumphantly, till Grandmomma
> said, *Shush, boy,* and I shushed.

In early versions of the poem, the versions closest to actual events, the person who calls the chickens poisonous is my aunt, not my grandmother. But having three characters in the poem—aunt, grandmother, me—complicated the scene unnecessarily and left the poem diffuse and unfocused. When I merged aunt and grandmother into one character, the scene snapped into artistic and dramatic coherence, and I was able to finish the poem. It was, I believe, a good aesthetic decision, one well worth the sacrifice of literal truth.

The problem with the lie of narrative cogency is that in life the stories *don't* stand clear of the underbrush; the flowering crab apple is obscured by sumac. So even this white lie falsifies experience: intensification and clarity *are* misrepresentations. But I've listened to so many well-intentioned friends agonize to get pointless facts straight that I don't worry about this lie too much: "In the third grade, Miss Porter hit me with a ruler for . . . No, wait—I think it was the fourth grade because Daddy hadn't yet bought the green Plymouth. But, then, maybe I'm confusing Uncle Ralph's green Dodge with Daddy's Plymouth. He—Daddy, I mean—really loved that car. . . . " Torture by exactitude.

2. If the lie of narrative cogency contracts, condenses, tightens memory, the lie of texture expands it. Some details of course are welded forever into our memories: how Grandmother smelled of Vicks VapoRub, the way Mother always mispronounced "municipal" as "mu-NINCE-ipal," then mocked herself for not being able to say it properly. But most details slide out of our memories because they aren't important until we try to write about the past, and then they are essential because storytelling thrives on details, which enrich the texture of bare plot. The accumulation of precise and telling details is what makes the story, scene, image, line vivid in the reader's imagination, while memory tends to drop details and preserve the emotional reaction they evoked. So, in order to capture the reality of an experience, I was, in an odd paradox, sometimes forced to invent details to make it more believable.

A small for instance: in "Funeral Parlor Fan" I wrote about a handheld fan of the sort that's very popular in rural, unairconditioned churches. On one side the fan has a sentimental picture of Jesus and on the other an advertisement for a local funeral home.

> I fanned
> a little more, grew bored, and jabbed
> my brother, kicked the seat in front of me
> till, casually, my mother's hand
> dipped out and popped my head, not hard,
> with Jesus praying in the garden
> or, flipped, Hobb's Funeral Home. And just
> to hear myself talk, I'd say *ouch*
> and get another dose of Jesus,
> and slightly harder too. The beat
> resumed: tick tock, tick tock, and I
> took up the worn, two-sided fan
> and tried—small hands—to keep the beat.
> Tick: Jesus. Tock: Hobb's Funeral Home.

Though the poem says *Hobb's* Funeral Home, I can't remember what funeral home actually supplied fans to the Vineyard Baptist Church. I needed a one-syllable word and, after much flipping through books looking at names, I chose Hobb. As many hours as I sat in church, reading and rereading the back of those fans, you'd think I'd remember the name emblazoned in huge letters on them. You'd think I'd remember the name of the people who buried one of my grandfathers, both grandmothers, two uncles, one cousin, and my mother. But I don't, and this particular poem would sound unconvincing and I would sound moronic if I jerked it to a halt and admitted my ignorance.

3. The lie of fictional convention. While every word of "When I Was Saved" is literally true, I can't help feeling that this poem about my being born again and baptized into the Southern Baptist Church, because of its subject, meshes too easily with what readers anticipate when they read a book subtitled *A Southern Childhood*. Religion, anguish, sweat, guilty sex, and physical deformity are, after all, characteristics of Southern writing that readers are accustomed to expect:

> I couldn't breathe at all
> when I, damp handkerchief clamped on my mouth,

was lowered into death. I went down easy,
stayed, panicked, struggled, and was yanked back up,
red-faced and dripping. After that, each Sunday
I went to preaching early so I could sit
behind a boy whose torn right ear did not
attach entirely to his head. Through that
pink gap of gristle, I'd watch the preacher shout,
croon, soothe—between that boy's head and his ear.
More sinners lumbered up the aisle. I longed
to run up and again be purged of Adam,
who was reborn each night, like Lazarus,
by my own hand, beneath the sweat-drenched sheets.

I worry that I may have traded on elements in my life that I've come to understand are exotic to readers who did not grow up in evangelical Christian churches. One of the most disconcerting things about writing an autobiography was seeing my life, which I'd preferred to think of as unique, take on recognizable literary conventions. The autobiographer takes his or her own life as material and, once it is material, it, for some purposes, stops being life and becomes primarily material. Then it falls into categories of material, like the coming-of-age story or the Southern grotesque. I suddenly looked up from the page I was writing and saw myself not as myself, an individual, but as a character in a poem fathered by William Faulkner and carried to term by Flannery O'Connor.

Questions arise: Did they teach me to see what I see or did they teach me how to write about what I see? Or did we all drink from the well of common cultural experience? I prefer to believe the last possibility, but I suspect it's a combination of the three. One thing I don't point out in the poem, though, is that my conversion and baptism took place not in Alabama, but in San Bernardino, California, while my father was stationed at nearby Norton Air Force Base.

4. The lie of emotional evasion. The sin of omission. The things that make us evasive and shifty in life are the things we will attempt to slide over on the page. Sex and death are the deep sources of most euphemism and avoidance—as well as other forms of emotional flinching, ducking, dodging, fudging, and sidestepping. Though we'll write about actions we were

ashamed of once but have since come to terms with, the actions and attitudes we remain ashamed of are hard to put on the page. It's difficult for me to say what I'm evasive about. If I had been deliberately evasive about something while writing the book, I'd probably still want to sidestep it; and since many evasions are self-deceptions, how can I admit to ducking a subject I'm unaware of ducking?

If I recognized that I wanted to slide over something, I made myself go right at it. One source of evasion that's especially sensitive to a Southerner is our culture's touchiest taboo at the moment: race. It's a subject that I'd tried to write about for decades, but I'd always failed. It overwhelmed anything I could say about it. It seemed to overwhelm language itself. But since I knew overlooking racism would be dishonest, I forced myself to write about it. Though I'm generally pleased with the poems that resulted, I learned that it takes a lot of energy to blast through the resistance to writing about difficult and painful subjects, and, as a consequence, the things I don't want to say are the things I say harshest and loudest. I'm afraid I may have overemphasized the anguish, unhappiness, and sorrow I felt as a child trying to come to terms with—trying to *understand*—the past and present racism of the world around me.

I don't think I was evasive about death. I've been obsessed with death since I was a child and if anything I give it too much attention in the book. But I was evasive about sex, and not because I'd enjoyed such a rollicking adolescence that I didn't want to brag or that I wished to spare the reputations of my many lovers. Rather the opposite. Raised Southern Baptist, a faith I took seriously even as I was seriously troubled by it, I didn't, in fact, have sex till I was married. (Well, depending on exactly how one defines sex.) But on the few occasions I've shared that fact with friends I've either been called a liar to my face or marveled at with polite and amused sympathy. It took many attempts before I was able to mention, quickly and in passing, that my first sexual experience took place on my wedding night, and I only put it in the book because I felt I had to.

5. Emotional evasion is merely the first step on the path that leads to the considerably more egregious lie of the recreated

self. When I, as a teenager, began to write, one of my first discoveries was that I could make myself look good. This temptation is, of course, an extension of the human tendency to recount events so our motives are clear, understandable, noble, while other people's are left unexamined or put in a bad light. And in writing, with the opportunity to explain ourselves even more fully and thoughtfully, as well as to shade or shape facts, circumstances, and actions, it's easier yet to make ourselves the heroes of our own lives. For about six months after this discovery, I was enthralled by how I could be so much wittier, shrewder, kinder, more sensitive, and more knowledgeable on the page than I am in life. I could be the me I'd always wanted to be—and without doing the hard work of attaining the virtues I claimed for myself. But it was sleazy, this self-ennobling, and I knew it was sleazy. Soon I reacted against it, and vowed I wouldn't do it anymore. Maybe because I was once so in love with how I could present the reader with a new and improved version of myself, I react with almost physical revulsion when I suspect a writer is gilding his blemishes. My wife says I now take a perverse delight in putting unnecessarily ugly constructions on my own motives. Perhaps she's right. The truth is, being wrong, flawed, crude, ungracious, and incomplete is pretty much the story of my life. But it's also true that presenting myself on the page as such packs an emotional kick for both writer and reader.

Consider how I come across in "The Colonel":

> My father lifts the crippled airman's body
> and jokes about how light he is and how
> we need some rain. He holds him while the man's
> young wife strips off the yellowed linen, cracks
> white sheets above the bed and lets them drift
> across the mattress. She smooths them, tucks the corner.
> My father lays the shriveled Christian down.
> Three times one week, four times the next. A job
> he shares with someone from another church.
> He comes home ashen. And every single time,
> before he leaves the house he turns to me,
> false casually, "You want to come along?"

"Do you need help?" I ask, and he says no.
He leaves. I watch teevee. I'm sixteen, shit!
And I don't want to be a soldier yet.

In the poem I refuse to assist my father in a disagreeable but noble task, though I do imply that if he'd said my help was necessary I'd have obliged. But I did prettify my actions. As I wrote about this incident, it seemed to me to show the sullen refusal of an adolescent to embrace cheerfully the responsibilities of adulthood and the obligation to serve others, so I changed my age in the poem to sixteen. Actually I was in my late twenties, living briefly with my father after my first marriage had failed and I was between jobs. Even when making ourselves look bad we can still find a way to make ourselves look good. "Gilding our blemishes," I called it a few paragraphs ago, when I was scorning others for doing it.

6. Lies of extended consciousness. This mystical-sounding category covers two kinds of lies. One is the outright appropriation of other people's experiences. Theft. But it's not really theft, the thief protests. The story was just lying around and John Reese wasn't using it. He's in the Air Force now. What's he going to do with his story? Besides, I need it more than he does. I can put it to use. And in "The Benedictine Hand" I put to use my friend's story about his high school biology teacher who, while showing the class how to insert a glass tube into a rubber stopper, slipped and jabbed the tube into her palm:

> "Now that's what you are not supposed to do,"
> she said. She held two frozen fingers up,
> as if to bless us. "I've cut the median nerve.
> This is what's called the Benedictine Hand.
> It's paralyzed." She flexed her thumb and last
> two fingers. The blessing fingers stayed erect.
> Then, pale, she wrapped her red hand in a wad
> of towels, left the room —quick, angry steps.

As I say, I didn't see this happen. My friend John Reese saw it, a boy who was enough like me, I'm tempted to argue, that it makes little essential difference that he saw it and I didn't. Not only could I have easily been the boy who saw his teacher ram a jagged glass tube into her palm, I know exactly which one of my own teachers would have done it and how she would have reacted. Since the day in the Huntingdon College dining room when John told me the story, Mrs. Houston has so many times in my imagination driven that tube into her palm and stood before the class with blood trickling down her left wrist and forearm that I can only with great difficulty remember that it's not a memory.

After *The Glass Hammer* was published, I called John and apologized for stealing his story. He didn't know what I was talking about. He'd forgotten. Which only proves that the story was more important to me than it was to him and thus rightly mine because I realized its true value. Is it really stealing, the thief asks, if the victim doesn't miss it when it's taken?

A more subtle, less clearly transgressive form of the lie of extended consciousness occurs when the writer applies knowledge he or she has as an adult to a childhood experience. That's what I do in "Fireflies After Twilight," in which I reflect on being a boy sleeping on a screened-in porch, watching fireflies till I fell asleep:

> Rarely more
> than one light quavered at a time,
> flicking its diminishing sexual light
> against the crowded pines. Eros
> and Thanatos I'll call it now
> but then I simply called it fear.
> If I'm still frightened—and I am—
> it's complicated with yearnings
> toward doubleness and indecision:
> how during sunlight I block light,
> which warms my back and loosens me,
> while after dark I stand out, white
> against the black pines, usually
> but not always at odds with nature,
> God and the gods. . . .

I am almost as different from that child I once was as I am from John Reese. Just as I stole John's story, I am in this poem stealing a story from my young self and using it for my adult reflections—

reflections that would baffle and annoy the ten- or twelve-year-old boy who lived the experience. Ten or twelve. See? I don't even know him well enough to know how old he is. The adult interprets that boy's life in ways the boy would not comprehend and would probably reject out of hand as making a big deal out of nothing.

And now we have already moved deeply into the next lie.

7. The lie of interpretation. The essential lie. When I was about three-quarters of the way through *The Glass Hammer*, I sent what I'd written so far to my editor, Peter Davison, a writer with a clear eye for writing and the ability to make himself excruciatingly clear even to those who have ears and cannot hear.

"The book doesn't go anywhere," he said.

"Yeah, I know. I don't want it to. If the book ended with a forced sense of reconciliation, it'd be a lie."

"I didn't say it should have a forced sense of reconciliation. I said it didn't go anywhere."

"Life doesn't go anywhere. That's the point."

"It's unsatisfying to read a book that just stops. As it is now, your manuscript just drops off the table. Think about how you'd feel if you were reading it."

And finally what friends had been trying to tell me for almost a year became crystal clear. My vow to write while I was still angry had brought me this far but it was now making it impossible for me to end the book. "I was pissed off then and I'm still pissed off now, but at least I can laugh about it" isn't much in the way of making one's life comprehensible to a reader. That's a truth I normally have a firm grasp on but I'd let it slip from my hands while grappling with the psychological complexities that got churned up when I tried to turn my own personal life into literary material. Grudgingly I went back to work, trying to make sense out of material—my life!—that I had resisted making sense out of because first I'd have to understand it, and that understanding could be tentative, provisional, and painful. Then I'd have to forgive it, which is painful. Then I'd have to ask for forgiveness, which is even more painful. Then I'd have to write it all down through many drafts, which means going through the whole ordeal over and over again. Aesthetics and psychology are uncomfortably interwoven, but in autobiography the warp and woof is pulled even tighter than in most fiction because the writer's own emotional, spiritual, and intellectual progress becomes the aesthetic progress of the book.

But was I wrong to resist meaning, resolution, closure? Interpretation *is* the lie of tendentiousness. We live our lives, most of us, ambivalent, full of unresolved emotions and guilts, unsure of where we're going and where we've been, and, more unnervingly, unsure of why we're where we are. But all that suspended feeling and thought, if it remains suspended, makes for an unsatisfying aesthetic experience. The problem boils down to this: life has no intrinsic meaning while art has to have it. Or at least significance. Or, if not significance, shape. The biographer is given a natural closure for his or her book—death. But the autobiographer, being alive, has to choose where to end. That act of choice, an aesthetic decision, then echoes throughout the rest of the book, modifying and shedding light and dark on all that has come before, more like the end of a novel than the end of a biography, more like the closing of a fictional world than the end of one life in the continuing flow of history.

The greatest poem about childhood is Wordsworth's *The Prelude,* a poem I hated from the moment I began reading it. I hated it not as a poem. As a poem, it's magnificent. I hated it as a romantic and romanticized view of childhood. Stephen Gill, in his fine biography of Wordsworth, returns time after time to Wordsworth's poetic account of his own childhood, pointing out where the poet is being interpretative—where he violates chronology, where he is evasive, and where it's impossible to discern if he's being literally accurate, as he shapes his story to demonstrate how nature was the dominant force in his childhood. Almost everything that does not support this thesis is swept away or suppressed.

Reading Gill on Wordsworth and *The Prelude,* I finally understood I didn't hate the poem; I simply hated Wordsworth's interpretation of childhood, and was not yet willing to grant him his interpretation of his own childhood. My temperament is not romantic, and if I hated many Southern memoirs, no matter how well written, for their soft-focus sentimentality toward childhood, happy families, and the Fair Sex, I loved Maxim Gorky's *Childhood* and *Adolescence* for their harsh, gritty view of those same things. But Gorky lied too. Interpreted. His grittiness is often in the service of his Marxism, as is Richard Wright's in *Black Boy*. Not that Gorky's, Wright's, or Wordsworth's interpretations are necessarily wrong. It's just that they *are* interpretations, and thus, like most interpretations, exclusive. Like St. Augustine's interpretation of his life, Jonathan Edwards's of his, Rousseau's of his, and Benjamin Franklin's of his. And once we've posited a reading of our lives, we tend to look back and see how all roads could only have led us to the truth because it *is* the truth, and all roads could only have led us to where we are because here we are. A formulated interpretation tends to drive out other possibly valid interpretations and suppress ambivalence, ambiguity, and chance. But if having an interpretation presents aesthetic difficulties, not having one, as I finally came to see, presents more. Even worse than the overdetermined, moralizing story is the story with no reflections, no point, no sense of progress—emotionally, intellectually, or spiritually. If we are listening to a story, there has to be a reason the story is being told and a reason we're listening.

My vow to stay angry was of course an interpretation too, but the premature interpretation of a fifteen-year-old boy, and as I thought about it I began to see why the memoirists that I'd been angry with, and contemptuous of, had striven so hard—often too hard—to forgive and be forgiven. The rage of a sullen and oversensitive boy is unattractive but appropriate at fifteen; in the mouth of a forty-two-year-old man it's the immature product of a stunted personality. And I would have deprived my book of any forward movement at all if, out of fidelity to the vow of a fifteen-year-old boy, I had omitted the understanding I'd struggled to acquire over the intervening twenty-seven years. Still, I'm satisfied that some—enough—of my adolescent anger, confusion, and unhappiness came through in the finished book anyway. *The Glass Hammer* was recently included on the Young Adult Library Services Association's "list of recommended books for young readers" because it was "identified as having high appeal for teens, ages 12–18, who, for whatever reasons, do not like to read"—an honor I'm still mulling over, pleasure wrestling with bafflement for the upper hand.

8. While interpretation lies by saying "It means this," impres-

sionism lies by saying "It feels like this." Reading over my own book, I was surprised by how my childhood came across as very rural, very country. Because my father was a career military man, I lived in Texas, New Mexico, England, Ohio, North Carolina, California, and France before he was stationed in Montgomery, Alabama, where, as I mentioned, he retired and where I attended high school and college. But both my parents grew up in Griffin, Georgia, and when they could they took me and my brothers back there to spend time in the country with my grandmother, aunts, and uncles, as well as first, second, and third cousins arrayed in gradations of kinship that I could never comprehend. Even more important than our visiting Griffin, though, is the way my parents carried rural Georgia with them wherever they went, and from them I absorbed country expressions, speech patterns, attitudes, beliefs, and habits of thought without even knowing I was absorbing them. The book may give an impression of a more rural childhood that the one I actually lived, but it does give a true reflection of one way I perceived my life, a true reflection of how large those visits to Georgia loomed in my memory and imagination.

I'm always astonished at how falsely I remember things, astonished at how plastic memory is. And even when I know a memory is incorrect, part of my brain cleaves to the wrong, imagined memory, and now I hold two images in my head, two memories—and the false one is more vivid and more emotionally significant to me than the actual one. Which, then, is the truest memory? It's convenient when the actual events adequately convey the emotional experience, but sometimes they don't and the writer has to choose. I acknowledge the dilemma in a poem about my grandfather's funeral:

> A week from now I'd start
> to wonder where Da-daddy was. I'd ask.
> Momma would hug me, moan, try to explain.
> But in the hot car, now, her bright red lips
> churned wordlessly until they caught. She screamed.
> My father, cousins, kin all say I'm wrong.
> But that's how I remember it: she screamed.
> ("In a Car Outside the Vineyard Baptist Church")

While I wouldn't be so disingenuous as to argue that a false memory is valid simply because it is vivid, I would argue that there must be some subjective truth to it, some emotional truth—and that one reads an autobiography to see how the writer experienced and evaluates his or her life and a biography to find a more objective view. The lie of impressionism is the biggest lie, the least defensible logically, ethically, or morally; and it's inescapable for a writer attempting to create an artistically coherent work. Even appropriated memories, like the one about the teacher who stuck the glass tube through her hand, have an emotional force for the person who needed to appropriate them, and if that force is strong enough it's almost as misleading to omit them as it is to include them.

My argument grows strained and my tone shrill because I'm unhappy with the illogical, unethical, and immoral position that practical experience has led me to. But the trust I bring to reading an autobiography is a reader's trust in a convincingly told tale, not the trust I bring to reading the *New York Times* or a history of Assyria, in which aesthetics are secondary to factual accuracy. The autobiography dances on the shifting middle ground between fact and fiction, reportage and imagination, actuality and art; and different writers will draw their lines on that ground in different places. As an artist, a poet, I drew my line considerably further to the side of impressionism than a reporter or historian might have, or than I had meant to when I began the book.

Though the lies of interpretation and impressionism bother me, they are essential. We read memoirs precisely to find out what one writer thinks his life means and how that life felt to the one who lived it. As I look back over *The Glass Hammer,* I say, yes, that *is* what my childhood means, and, yes, that *is* how it felt. And, to make those two affirmations, I accept, however uneasily, the lies I had to tell.

III

Interview with Nick Norwood

Interview with Nick Norwood

NN: You're a member of a long tradition of poets and fiction writers whose use of language is sometimes characterized as biblical. But even in your most biblical poems, poems like "Amen" and "Consider," your language maintains a sort of modern leanness and athleticism. How do you strike that balance and how would you characterize the difficulty of the modern poet in maintaining a connection to the language of the Bible?

AH: Two of my uncles were Methodist ministers and I, being Southern Baptist, was surrounded by preachers—people of The Word and people who were admired for their ability to bring people to The Word. In Southern Baptist churches, there is a lot of storytelling and verbiage cascading from pulpits, and it all has designs on you. The purpose of all that passionate, driven language, with its dizzying swerves between the biblical, the Elizabethan, and the colloquial, is to get you out of your seat. Its goal is to get you to walk down the aisle, accept Jesus, be baptized, and join the church—all of which I did. It's emotionally manipulative toward an intellectual, moral, pragmatic end, and the fact that the manipulation is meant for your own good by people who are generally honest and sincere doesn't make it any less manipulative. Maybe more.

Naturally I reacted against lush rhetoric, exaggeration, emphatic moralizing, and the sentimentality that tends to underlie all that stuff. I worked very hard and consciously to write in a lean language, with a tight line to keep the rhetorical temptations under control. But biblical language and cadences are

From *Hayden's Ferry Review* 16 (Spring/Summer 1995): 9–27.

marrow deep in my sense of what language can do—or even *is*—and I doubt I could purge that entirely from my writing and talk if I wanted to. And now I don't. The two imperatives exist in a tension that I hope is a happy one.

That shifting sharply back and forth across levels of diction—even histories of diction—that I heard in sermons is something I love in writing for the amplitude it offers. It makes the work bigger because of the different perspectives it implies, and the shift from tone to tone enlarges the emotional depth of the poem simply because it makes the reader aware of more emotions in the poem. That's the way I talk, that's the way *you* talk, that's the way everybody I know with any self-consciousness toward language talks. But, damn, it's hard to get right on the page. Byron is a genius at it. And Pope and Dickens. George Eliot, Henry Fielding, and Sir Thomas Browne, whom I adore. The play of intelligence through tone and tonal shift vastly complicates and expands the ideas that it is entertaining.

NN: You've said publicly that Southerners are notorious blowhards and that you're guilty of it too. Do you attribute any of your success as a poet to this aspect of your southernness?

AH: Sure, Southerners are terrible gasbags. And I can bore a crowd to stupefaction with the best of them, telling stories and jokes.

The South is a social culture and a courtesy culture. Courtesy *demands* that you have a social exchange with the people you deal with, and that means you have to *talk* to the clerk ringing up your canned tomatoes at the Piggly Wiggly. When my family moved back to the South, I, at fourteen, found the whole thing intimidating: I didn't know what to say to the complete stranger who, while ringing up my candy bar, asked what I thought about Alabama's chances versus Tennessee that weekend. How the hell should I know? But as I got used to it and began to play—and it is play—I began to see what else it was: a courtesy and, despite the formulaic nature (or because of it; ritual has its uses), an attempt to let the other person be real to you. Not merely "customer" or "neighbor" but "Guy who supports Tennessee" or "Woman who wants it to rain so her roses won't die." While that's not intimacy, it's a pleasant step away from nonentity.

In Tuscaloosa, in graduate school, I was nonplussed by the new Yankee professors and their spouses who'd sneer about store clerks and friendly neighbors, "Sure, they *seem* friendly, but they don't really want to *know* you." Though we said nothing to them at the time because that would of course be discourteous, I remember my wife saying later, "Jesus, the poor clerk is just trying to make a lousy job go pleasantly and they want her to bear their children."

So, like everyone, I learned that language and attention to the levels of meaning, stated and unstated, are vital in daily life.

NN: Your use of narrative structure and dramatic monologue obviously has an impact on the language in your poems. How would you describe that impact?

AH: A couple of years ago after I gave a reading in New York, there was a question-and-answer period, and a woman in the audience asked what was more important to me, story or words, though I think she actually said narrative or language. I tried to joke about the subject; she got annoyed, impatient, and snapped that I should answer the question. And I, in turn, snapped back "story" just because I figured, for no particular reason, that was the answer she would not approve of. But I've always regretted that I didn't have the presence of mind and emotional maturity—twenty-twenty hindsight—to say it's a false choice.

What would you rather hear, a poorly told story or gorgeous gibberish? Duh! Most people given such a choice would say, "Maybe I'll just take a long hot bath." But in the real world the answer is "Why can't I have a gorgeously told story?" If the choice is Dreiser or Swinburne, choose Dante, Chekhov, Faulkner.

But you're right of course about narrative structure and dramatic monologue influencing language. In most dramatic monologues you have to employ a more subdued language than in lyrical poetry since few people speak consistently in lyrical phrases, though they do, or can, rise to it on occasion. And though I love with an uneasy love lyricism and even high-flown rhetoric, I love most the cadences of a speaking voice and how those cadences, as well as diction and of course content, reveal psychological complexity.

From time to time I've tried to write in the third person but mostly I find that the distance from the character's thought processes and voices is hard for me to work with. And on a purely technical level I find it murderously difficult to keep the pronouns straight without lapsing into a prose precision that seems to a poet like a lot of dead syllables that undermine the tension of the line, especially if you're working in meter.

On the page and in real life, I'm fascinated by the movement of the voice as the speaker, like all speakers, reveals and hides, evades and confesses, dissembles and tells scorching truths—all the while wanting to be liked and respected, to get rich, to get laid, to keep from suffering—all at the same time. It's marvelous and flawed, "like most of we," as Berryman says in *The Dream Songs*.

Some writers talk about language as if it were God, perfect and purifying. That's absurd. Like any human creation, it has its virtues and its limitations. Others whine about language as an imperfect tool, which of course it is. But they assume, it seems to me, that language limits perception and understanding because it is too coarse an instrument to register all the minute twitches of sensibility or even that because of its structure it precludes some modes of thought entirely. Now all that may be true, but my sense is that if it weren't for language there would be precious few perceptions or understandings at all. And, too, a bad carpenter blames his tools. Just because I or you or Ethel Mertz can't state with exquisite precision every shift of ambivalence in our attitudes toward each other doesn't mean that Henry James can't.

Sure, language is imperfect, but so is every chisel, plane, and saw, no matter how well crafted, and chairs still get made and they still hold our butts up off the floor.

NN: I hear through reliable sources you're both a quilter and a gardener. There are a number of gardening poems in your earlier books, and there's a quilting poem in the new one. But besides providing material for your poems, what effect do these activities have on your writing?

AH: If I thought I was doing those things to write about them, I'd blow my brains out. That's backward. That's living your life so you'll have something to write about it. Do you fall in love for the subject matter? Well, we all know people like that, don't we?

But people who do that have miserable lives—consider the poets of the fifties—and they *should* have miserable lives so they can serve as a reminder to the rest of us to get the order right: horse first, then cart. Life first, then art.

I get a little vehement on the subject, probably because I'm inclined to be obsessive and need to remind myself of the importance of balance. I tend to get deeply involved in things for a while and go after them single-mindedly; then after a while I get bored and let them slide. At the moment there's a half-finished quilt in my hall closet and two partially assembled chairs on my workbench in the basement. At first I worried about how my interest would dwindle. I thought it meant I lack resolve or commitment or whatever. But then I realized, nah, I have certain core interests I'm dedicated to, but at times I need a respite and I'll get a bee in my bonnet, as my mother called it, to go off reading about woodworking, gardening, quilting, mutual funds, or whatever. It's fun to stumble into a new area and learn to appreciate it, to get a grasp on the existence of complexities, histories, and aesthetics I hardly knew existed. And it's fun to learn all those new words. It's a way of being interested in the world.

NN: Throughout your four books, and especially in the last two, one sees in many of the poems with Christian and biblical themes a curious combination of deeply religious sentiment and often highly irreverent language, including, in a few cases, scatological references. Obviously, this use of language carries a certain amount of shock value, but I sense you feel there's a value beyond that. Is there, and if so, how would you describe it?

AH: In high school or college, when I first sat down and from some impulse began doodling with words, the language of the Bible poured out of me—and with it came a fixation on religious questions. I was astounded and a bit embarrassed. I thought, then, I was a cold agnostic, superior to such concerns.

But the only great writing I'd been exposed to as a kid was the Bible, which I heard at church at least once a week, sometimes twice or three times; and during revivals with a traveling preacher we could be in church as many as five times a week. And my father read the Bible to us every night and led us in prayers. The only philosophical thinking I'd ever heard was in religious terms—Plato by way of St. Paul. So the only serious ways I knew to talk or think about the world were in biblical terms.

And because of that evangelical background the scatological words have a lot of impact for me. They are powerfully transgressive, violative, and clearly dangerous to the person saying them. In our house cursing was forbidden and punished furiously so you had to be very careful negotiating acceptable vocabulary. "Go potty" was okay; now let's see if I can get away with saying "poop." How about "dump" or "drop a load." That got a funny look from Dad; I'd better be careful. "Crap," at first wasn't okay, but later became edgily acceptable. "Defecate" he didn't like but he couldn't really complain about it because it was technical.

Another example: my father once smacked me good and hard for calling one of my brothers a fool. The Bible says something to the effect that a man who calls his brother a fool is in danger of hellfire. That made the word all the more tempting to say and more terrifying. And it made my father all the more terrified for my soul. When he hit me, he was hitting me both because I was violating a sense of family and community and courtesy and religion when I called Roger a fool, but I had also put my soul at risk of eternal damnation and he was frightened for me. And for years I believed that the unforgivable sin was saying "goddamn." That merely voicing those two syllables was a shortcut to hell.

So those words, sacred and profane, not only have a lot of resonance for me, but are strongly linked to one another, dependent on one another.

NN: There are a number of references to popular culture in your poems and your use of language often reflects your exposure to it, which— unlike many of your contemporaries who might complain of an involun-

tary exposure—you don't seem to resent or resist. Is that a fair assessment, or do you actually feel some discomfort over the degree to which the popular media affects your writing?

AH: What can I say? I'm a child of the mall and the TV set, as much as a child of the book, though books are my first and primary love. For all I've heard come from a living human throat I've probably heard ten times as much coming out of the simulated humans on TV or coming, completely disembodied, from the radio. To deny these things is to deny the world most of us are living in, but neither should they be loved too much.

One of my favorite too-often-told stories is that when I was at Stanford as a Stegner fellow Simone di Piero asked the class who in the room felt there was a distinction between high art like, oh, Dante and Shakespeare and low art like Tom Clancy novels and *Friday the Thirteenth* movies. I was the only one who raised his hand and as I did a couple of people smiled at me with amused contempt for being a "high-art elitist." Then Simone asked if anyone in the class had actually seen a *Friday the Thirteenth* movie and again I was the only one who raised his hand.

But even if we shouldn't love popular culture too much, that doesn't imply that we can't or shouldn't love it at all. As a child I adored *Our Miss Brooks* with wonderfully smart-mouthed Eve Arden. From movie reruns, I had a major crush on Shirley Temple and an equally strong fixation on Hayley Mills later. She was succeeded in my affections by Barbara Feldon, Agent 99 on *Get Smart,* then by Barbara Bain on *Mission Impossible.*

The first thing I ever tried to write, other than class assignments, was a *Man from U.N.C.L.E.* story. I wrote a paragraph about the secret entrance to the secret underground headquarters and then realized I knew nothing at all about the wider world except what I'd seen on TV or read about in books and I couldn't hope to fill up a single page even though I *owned and loved* a plastic *Man from U.N.C.L.E.* spy briefcase with a built-in gun and a hidden, fake camera. It was a much-whined-for Christmas present.

I love *Cops.* My wife and I are big fans of *The Simpsons, Beavis and Butthead, Furniture on the Mend,* and gardening shows. And I'm devoted to my country videos and VH-1, MTV for the middle-aged. But TV is all entertainment. Even the news seems to me a species of entertainment, and I don't take any of it too seriously. *I Love Lucy,* though, possesses more intelligence, craft, and even genius than many literary masterpieces I've slogged through unhappily. One of the things high art steals from low art is the vitality to keep its deeper engagement with the human condition alive.

I get a real kick out of the ways high art and low art clash, but I'm more interested in how low art feeds into high art, can be appropriated by it or used for the intelligence and serious engagement it can bear. Or enliven. Or undermine in a productive way. I get a charge out of the transgressive power that can be released when the two come together. It's fun to try to find something serious, some pathos, in *The Munsters* and not just cheap irony, though, that has its uses too—and it's fun to put that combination of fun and inappropriate seriousness into blank verse, where most people don't expect it to fit.

I'll never forget the dissociative thrill I felt when I read *The Waste Land* for the first time and got to "London Bridge is falling down falling down falling down." It blew me away. Even though I was a dense and uncomprehending seventeen year old living in Montgomery, Alabama, I understood at some dim level below articulation that that line, that *move,* made the poem both serious and less serious, both undercut the poem and intensified it—and expanded its amplitude psychically, historically, emotionally, and musically. It just simply blew me away.

Writers—and not just writers—have to look in several different directions at once. We have to live in the world around us, the present, and grapple with it as hard as we can. But we have to look toward the future too to see if we can find the impersonal in our personal, the thing that will let us talk to people who will share some of our experiences but not the trappings of our moment. Here is where the difference between high art and low art lies, it seems to me, and in the fullness of time some high art will be revealed as low and vice versa. Looking at the past can show us what persists over time and what doesn't. We are Byron's future and Shakespeare's—at least in part—and they are writing to us as much as to their own age. We judge how well they succeed, and we can try to figure out how they succeed so we can try it too. Or reject it. Or modify it. Some writers can, perhaps, discover the wheel one day and build a Ford GT the next, but I'm not one of them.

NN: In The Glass Hammer, *the poem "Was" describes an experience everybody has as a child, repeating a word until you lose its spelling, and even sometimes its meaning, having the word become "mere music." As a poet, what's your take on this aspect of language development?*

AH: When I was a kid, I was terrified by the way words would dissolve if handled too insistently or roughly. It connected to my sense, though I could not have articulated it then of course, that the world, the whole of civilization, was fragile and would break beneath my hands if I weren't very, very careful. When I repeated, chanted, sang a single word till I was no longer even sure how to say it, much less what it meant, I could feel chaos and the abyss open up beneath me, and I was truly frightened out of my mind. So, of course, I kept doing it, sneaking back up to the edge and staring into the void.

But now that I have more faith in the resilience of language, it's fun to play with it, fun to feel words resist chaos, insist on their arbitrary and hallowed connection to the world and to meaning. And I greatly admire and slightly regret how difficult it is to break those sounds free of the meanings we have assigned to them—or the meanings we have inherited from our ancestors who assigned them to those sounds.

I love the sudden soaring into mere music you get in Stevens or nonsense songs just for the exuberant *play* of them. Or those passages in Rolling Stones or R.E.M. songs that are so cool because you're not sure what you're hearing, and once you do learn what they're saying they're a lot less cool and a lot less intriguing.

But on the page those sorts of things are harder to do because music and performance aren't there to carry them off and because the written page is much more tightly wedded to meaning than songs are. It's something that to my mind should be done sparingly and brilliantly or not at all.

On a larger level, I believe you have to have chaos—an awareness of chaos—in every poem, at least a glance into the abyss if not a protracted stare. But chaos is not our friend. Whether it wins the battle or not, the poem must resist chaos, even if that resistance takes the form of trying to blast through the void and out the other side. Chaos is not our friend, but it is our constant companion and sometime lover, and so we may as well be on friendly terms with it, whatever we may say about it behind its back.

NN: In the verse epilogue of The Glass Hammer *you address the cathartic nature of your experience in writing those autobiographical poems, as well as the sense of having betrayed a trust in writing so candidly about members of your family. To what extent is the poet responsible for the "truth" when writing from an autobiographical position?*

AH: That's a difficult question, one I've spun around in circles for a long time—and one that I actually had more qualms about while writing *After the Lost War* in the voice of Sidney Lanier. About two-thirds of the way through that book I suddenly found myself agonizing over the fact that my character, who was based on the historical figure Sidney Lanier, was doing, saying, and thinking things that the historical Sidney Lanier would never ever do, say, or think. My character Sidney Lanier would horrify the historical Sidney Lanier, and my intrusion into the life of a real person began to horrify me. How would I like it if a hundred years after my death, somebody decided to resurrect my name and stuff into my mouth words I'd never say?

Now, all along I'd seen the project as a historical novel in verse, not as a biography, and I was more or less consciously using Lanier as a mask to work through concerns of my own. And not a little because I think the historical Sidney Lanier was not terribly interesting and a bit of a prig. His *life* was extremely interesting to me, emblematic of lots of things: the war, the South, the poet in the South, the artist versus a world that doesn't value him, the poet in the nineteenth century, the poet who wants to live a normal and decent life, man in nature, man dying—to name some of them. But the man living that interesting life wasn't himself very interesting to me. So I changed him. But he was a real person, a man who'd lived an actuality that I was falsifying for my own purposes. It seemed terribly exploitative. Probably because it was.

I finally resolved the impasse I found myself in by saying crassly, "In for a penny, in for a pound. I've got too much time and effort in this project to quit now." I even tried to change the character's name to something made up, but that destroyed the book, the character, the whole connection to actuality that I did not want to give up, however much I violated it. So my apology to Lanier at the beginning of the book is not meant to be coy; it's a real apology, a real confession, a real statement of intent. And I haven't written a persona poem since I finished that book eight years ago.

With *The Glass Hammer*, the issues were different. I felt from the beginning that my life was my life and that I had every right to write about it as I saw fit. Though I did worry, even agonize, over how the book might hurt or disturb my family, that fear didn't become powerful till late in the writing of the book, and it became most acute right before the book was published. I guess I don't think of poems as public documents till they're in books. Few people see them when they're in journals, and those few don't include my family members.

The book, no, would not pass as truth in a court of law. Judge Wapner would be appalled. I falsified things throughout, sometimes for purely technical convenience. I reduced my three brothers to two and left all the action in Montgomery, instead of trying to indicate all the moves we made around the USA and abroad as an Air Force family. For instance, I even lied about some of the jobs I held in college because it would have been too complicated and too tedious to stop a poem and say, "Well, I know I said I worked all of college at the Piggly Wiggly, but in fact I had a lot of jobs over those four years and some of them did involve grocery work." That kind of literal accuracy, which I could insist on but not expect in prose nonfiction, both as a reader and a writer, merely seems overscrupulous and unnecessary to the truth of what I was trying to get at in those poems.

Toward the end of the writing of the book, I went back through the manuscript and falsified deliberately and drastically, changing names and relations, trying to preserve a vestige of anonymity for my family and to reduce the chances of my ass ending up in a courtroom.

Other things I wrote in the book cannot be defended well logically or with an easy conscience—like taking an incident from the life of a friend and telling the story as if it were mine just because I've thought about it so long that I've completely imagined it as mine and carry it in my mind as if it were memory. Besides he's now in the Air Force. It's not like he's going to *use* it. To show you how my self-justification operated.

But in a way that I cannot defend logically or comfortably, I'm satisfied that *The Glass Hammer* is the most truthful I've ever written because—this is the old and perhaps shopworn impressionist defense—it captures as well as I was capable of, with as much emotional precision as I could muster, what it was like to be the child I was. Do I find that defense inadequate, intellectually and morally? Yes. Do I believe it to the core of my being and stand behind the honesty of that book? Yes.

NN: Your early, uncollected poems are quite different from the poems appearing in your books. "The Whale," for instance, is a prose poem, and you experiment with other forms in some of the poems published in Chicago Review. *When did you adopt the more, what I'll call, direct style you're writing in now and how exactly did you turn that corner?*

AH: The prose poem you mention was actually an experiment I did when I was in the Writers' Workshop at Iowa, a class assignment—and by that time I'd already written about two-thirds of *Saints and Strangers* and nearly one-third of *After the Lost War,* so I was already pretty committed to the plain style. But I like to play around with other ways of writing to see if I can do them, to see if there's anything in them for me.

I didn't really start writing in the plain style till I was twenty-six or twenty-seven and back living in Montgomery, Alabama, and teaching part-time at three different colleges and working retail after having done graduate work at Alabama and Syracuse. (I didn't go to Iowa till I was thirty.) Knowing I wouldn't have to take my poems into class and make them run the gauntlet, I was finally able to lift my eyes from the technical skills I'd been working so hard to learn and to start grappling with content.

But a lot of that focusing on content grew out of a decision to see if I could write in meter.

In my despair at not getting published, not getting a good job, not getting anywhere with the inert poems I was writing, I asked myself for the first time if I would bother to read the poems I was writing if I hadn't written them. The answer was no. After I recovered from the shock of that answer—and it took a couple of not very pleasant months—I asked myself what were the characteristics of the poems I liked to read. The answer was poems with very strong rhythms, usually in meter, with a clean, quick, tight movement, often narrative, with the complexities in the tone, drama, and psychology, not in the syntax or allusions. Rhyme has never much interested me. Another thing that was going on was that up till then I'd written exclusively in free verse and I'd been resisting the growing realization that I had no reliable sense of what a free verse line was. I couldn't tell why free verse lines end where they do and what principles, other than intuition or appearance on the page or sheer arbitrariness, drive those decisions. My lines were all overintellectualized; there was nothing sensual in them, no rock and roll. They didn't have any boogie-woogie in their socks.

So I began writing in blank verse. Some people today talk about meter as if it were an elitist exercise, as if it were cabalistic knowledge passed down from the elders of the Republican party to their children, like jobs in investment banking. I'd learned the basics of meter by scanning almost the entirety of *The Canterbury Tales* for Dr. Woodrow Boyette's Chaucer class at Alabama. We proved, as I recall, that every single line Chaucer wrote is metrically regular. Dr. Boyette was apparently still smarting from Dryden's crack about Chaucer's numbers being rough, and every year he proved Dryden wrong. I learned to write in meter by reading Paul Fussell's *Poetic Meter and Poetic Form* and by looking up every damn word that I wanted to use that had more than two syllables in it because I couldn't hear where the accents fell. After a couple of weeks it started making sense to me.

Later, when I reread Fussell and noticed his saying that most pentameter lines use an adjective to generate at least one beat—or something along those lines—I decided to start writing in an iambic tetrameter line just to see if I could cut some adjectives and, thus, some rhetorical flourishes out of my lines. Also the shorter line allows jazzier line breaks. I still love that tetrameter blank verse with all my heart.

And when I started to write in meter, my content, without my realizing it at first, began to change. I began to work more in narrative. I began to use more dialogue, more humor, and I began to include sharp tonal shifts and leaps of logic. The pulse of the meter gave me confidence that it could carry those things without collapsing into prose—a pressure that exposition and the plain style place heavily on free verse, which to my ear always bears the burden of proving it is poetry; therefore its bias is toward song and it cannot bear much talking. And once rhythm and line breaks became technical rather than intellectual decisions for me, they became sensual elements. I was able to move with the rhythm and trust it to carry me, and that, paradoxically enough, freed me to work with content in a way I hadn't been able to before.

Of course I understand very well that meter doesn't work that way for everyone. In my classes, I always ask everybody to write one poem in blank verse or iambic tetrameter. Some people are transformed; the meter picks them up and puts them down in a new and better place. It gives them access to areas of their intellect or of their sensuality—or both—that they'd been blocked from. And for others it's a horrible straitjacket that makes them look like clumsy bumblers and turns language and rhythm into enemies instead of friends. But I think they learn a lot from doing the exercise, even if all they learn is the exercise never becomes real to them and that they don't ever want to do it again.

NN: You use a lot of Southern expressions in your poems, not just for color, I suspect, but also as a way of examining language in general. "Threats and Lamentations" is a good example. How did hearing such threats and lamentations growing up affect your development as a poet?

AH: I love—most people do—a well-turned phrase whether it's by Oscar Wilde, Dorothy Parker, or the guy selling me two pounds of seed potatoes. But I detest writers who take those local phrases and use them for local color. It's condescending and sentimental to the point of viciousness to treat yourself and those around you as exotics.

I detest Southerners who put on the corn pone. When I was an undergrad at Huntingdon College in Montgomery, a building downtown burned down, and one of the business professors referred to the fire as "selling it to the Yankees." He meant that the business hadn't been doing well and he figured that the owner had torched the building to get the payoff from the insurance company, which was almost certainly not a Southern company. There are a lot of writers who take shopworn visions of the South—either of Stark Young's *Yellow Rose of Memphis* sentimentality or its reverse in the unrelieved squalor of Erskine Caldwell—and sell them to the Yankees. I try very hard not to sell corrupt, used, and useless goods to the Yankees. It corrupts the writer and demeans the reader to pretend the world is simpler than it is, whether you pretend it is better than it is or worse.

Even in those threats my mother made—I'll tan your bottom, I'll blister your behind, I'll slap you silly—there's a pleasure in the language that was clear at the time to the adult threatening violence and clear in retrospect to the child being threatened. The message is of course mixed. The words mean "I'm going to hit you," but the tone says, "This is just a preliminary threat, and you'd better stop while I'm in a semi-teasing mood because if you don't you'll get smacked for real."

But, you know, there's only one word in that poem I think of as Southern, and that's the use of "boy" to remind me of my place as a child—and it also indicates, in the undertones, affection and amusement.

Those threats are just things I was told as a child and I have no real idea to what extent they are Southern as opposed to, say, Western, or if they occur more frequently in military families, or if they are idiosyncratic to my family.

How did these things affect me as a poet? I'm not sure. But I've always been fascinated—as a very young child and as a writer and as a reader—by the gap between what is said and what is meant—and how that gap is manipulated by both speaker and listener, writer and reader.

NN: You've said you don't read other poets when you're composing poems. What do you read during those times and what are your reading/work habits when you're writing new poems?

AH: A couple of months ago I was reading *Don Juan* and I was completely enthralled by it, but after a while I had to stop because I kept wanting to be Byron, to write *Don Juan*—something my talents, such as they are, are utterly unsuited to. My sensibility became so tuned to that poem, so *surrendered* to it (to use T. S. Eliot's term), that I had to stop reading it just so I could get some writing done.

I tend to go back and forth—reading a lot of poetry when I can't write and reading prose when I'm writing poetry. It keeps things a little cleaner. It keeps Byron from seeping into what I do in too raw a fashion.

A lot of my reading is determined by my writing projects. When I was writing *After the Lost War* I read a lot of Civil War stuff—novels, memoirs, journals, histories. And even when I read about, say, World War II, I found details I could adapt for my book or modes of thinking I could adapt for my character. When I was writing *The Never-Ending* I read a lot of books about Christ and about art. And when I was writing *The Glass Hammer* I read tons of autobiographies and books about autobiography. From Southern autobiographies with their pervasive sentimentality (Mama was a saint, Uncle Bubba a kindly drunk, we was poor but proud, etc.), I mostly learned what I didn't want to do—and the aristocratic alternative was never an option open to me. But from the Russians—Tolstoy, Gorky, and others—as well as from strange books like Edmund Gosse's *Father and Son,* I got a much surer sense of how to write about love with open eyes—or even how to love with open eyes.

But now, between projects, I'm just reading what catches my eye. Earlier this year I was on a world war riff: the first two volumes of a projected three volume biography of Robert Graves by his nephew, followed by Graves's own *Goodbye to All That,* followed by Fussell on World War I and II, then a book on World War II in film by Tom Doherty. Lately, I've somehow got on a nineteenth-century novel jag, reading *Pickwick Papers, Melmoth, The Monk,* etc. I don't know why. One of the great advantages of being an artist as opposed to a scholar is that you don't have to read systematically or exhaustively.

I'm sort of drifting now—fingering the threads, studying the tea leaves—trying to figure out what comes next. And when I do, my reading will take on a bit more shape. I hate being in between projects, but I love when you get to the place in a project when it starts to generate its own momentum—when every book leads to another book and every poem leads to another poem—and everything you read, hear, see, and smell becomes grist for the mill.

NN: The racial tensions present in the Montgomery of your youth figure prominently in The Glass Hammer, *and in* The Never-Ending *the poem "The Unpromised Land," in which you adopt the persona of an office worker in Montgomery, addressing the protest marches occurring there in the sixties; but no poems on the marches appear in* The Glass Hammer. *That's a conspicuous absence, isn't it? I sense some indication in "The Unpromised Land" of how you feel about those events now, but what was your reaction to them at the time?*

AH: The persona of that poem is actually a sort of combination of me and my ex-wife. I was thinking about a job I'd had in downtown Montgomery as a sample clerk during my first year in college. "Sample Clerk" is what I found out my job was officially called after the company moved to Atlanta and I applied for unemployment, which for some reason or other I didn't get. What my job mostly consisted of was cutting cloth samples into little pinked squares and gluing them on display folders for salesmen to show to retail store owners. On breaks and at lunchtime, I'd walk to the capitol and back, stretching my legs and thinking about the rich unhappy history of my town. Later, when we moved back home after graduate school stints at Alabama and Syracuse, my ex-wife had a couple of jobs downtown, one as a lawyer for Legal Services; and I tried to imagine what it might mean for her to work downtown in this town where, with the exception of those four years in Tuscaloosa and Syracuse, she'd lived all her life—something that was hard for me to grasp because I was a military brat, and I didn't get to Montgomery till my first year of high school, in 1965, well after King had left town and the major marches were over. Integration began my second year of high school and there were, so far as I know, only a couple of larger "incidents" to highlight the various small insults and indignities the black students were subject to that year.

The only march I remember was the Klan's countermarch, when a couple of dozen of those pathetic losers marched from Selma to Montgomery and during the final leg of the march, into downtown Montgomery, they were outnumbered both by the people, black and white, protesting their march and by the police who were trying to keep the fairly violent crowd from attacking a frightened-looking bunch of Klan Klods, who seemed bewildered by the reaction they'd provoked. At least that's what it looked like to me on the TV.

I'd wanted to write about some of those racial issues for a long time but they overwhelmed me. They even seemed to me to overwhelm language. They were so difficult and wrenching, so charged, that they seemed to shrivel language or make it slide off into banalities. The idea of simply screaming "This is wrong, this is wrong" seemed obvious—not worth repeating in a poem. I'm about as interested in the political ruminations of poets, including my own, as I am in the literary ruminations of politicians. And the temptation to fall into a slow-motion spasm of self-preening sanctimony over one's sensibility to other people's suffering is all too tempting. It took me a long time and a lot of work before I could find a way around, or through, those obstacles, a way to write about my own implication in the racial past of my hometown.

But I'll tell you one reason poets avoid writing about racial subjects in anything but banalities. A friend of mine, a good poet too, declared as soon as she saw it, that that poem was racist, and I was so hurt that I didn't talk to her for a year. The poem depicts racism, yes, but any suggestion that the poem is endorsing what it depicts is just wrong. And after my last book came out, one old friend wrote and accused me of abusing blacks by using the word "nigger," although every single time that word is used it's used in dialogue and the "I" of the book is clearly disturbed by it. When it comes to race, because it's a taboo subject, I've found that even experienced readers are apt to confuse depicting racism with endorsing it. In the third act of *The Diary of Anne Frank*, the Nazis come and take Anne to Bergen-Belsen; that doesn't mean the playwright thinks it's a good idea.

NN: Both in terms of style and content, what direction do you see your poetry taking from here?

AH: Beats me. I feel like, after writing *The Glass Hammer,* I'm back to first principles, back to where I was before I wrote the poems that became my first book. Right now I'm sorting the threads, beating the bushes, trying to find the path that feels right beneath my feet. It's far from an intellectual process, though intellect can tell the intuition which paths to look at, consider, take a step or two down. But I don't want to make a decision that doesn't feel right and get committed to it and then have to bull it through, if I could, with sheer will. When a project is forced you can just smell, from two miles away, the stink of unadulterated will rising from the carcass.

So right now I'm doing a little of this, a little of that, resisting the impulse to make a damn decision and force myself into a shotgun wedding with it. I'm trying some free verse, some humor, some rhyme, snippets of allegory, some high-flown language. I'm even, god help us, doing some prose. I hate working so slowly and tentatively. If I don't have clear work—clear *writing* work—to do, I feel lazy and at loose ends. But *The Glass Hammer* took me as far as I could go with anger and humor. It wore me out, emotionally and artistically, and that's what it was supposed to do.

UNDER DISCUSSION
David Lehman, General Editor
Donald Hall, Founding Editor

Volumes in the Under Discussion series collect reviews and essays about individual poets. The series is concerned with contemporary American and English poets about whom the consensus has not yet been formed and the final vote has not been taken. Titles in the series include: